Donne's Petrarchism:
A Comparative View

by
SILVIA RUFFO-FIORE
University of South Florida

GRAFICA TOSCANA
FIRENZE - 1976

Grafica Toscana s.a.s. Firenze - Febbraio 1976

For my beloved Mafdi
In tribute to the years
1961-1975

PREFACE

This book is the result of research begun while I was a doctoral candidate at the University of Pittsburgh, continued on a Fulbright-Hays grant at the University of Rome, and ultimately completed and refined while teaching at the University of South Florida. It represents a compilation of four articles already published, two papers presented at scholarly conferences, and three new major essays. The book's main purposes are [1] to present a textual analysis of Donne's *Songs and Sonnets* in terms of how they relate to Petrarch's *Canzoniere*,[2] to define more clearly the nature of Donne's Petrarchism,[3] to suggest ways in which Donne deviated from Petrarch's style and love ethic. The book does not intend to show direct influence, but simply to offer a reading of Donne which takes into account one of the most profound and pervasive literary forces of the Renaissance.

I would like to thank the editors of *Comparative Literature, Comparative Literature Studies, Forum Italicum,* and *Italian Quarterly* for permission to include essays already published. My gratitude extends as well to my family, my dear mother who died in 1971, my father, my sister, Antoinette, and my nephew, Michael, for the pride they have so often shown in my work, the praise and encouragement they have freely given. To Mafdi, my beloved husband and devoted friend, I owe the inspiration for each word herein printed.

ACKNOWLEDGMENTS

Chapter I originally appeared as " The Unwanted Heart in Petrarch and Donne," *Comparative Literature* (Fall, 1972), 319-327; Chapter II as " Donne's ' Parody' of the Petrarchan Lady," *Comparative Literature Studies* (December, 1972), 392-406; Chapter V as " A New Light on the Suns and Lovers in Petrarch and Donne," *Forum Italicum* (December, 1974), 546-556; Chapter VI as " Donne's Transformation of Petrarchan Imagery in ' The Canonization '," to appear in 1976 in *Italian Quarterly*. Chapter VII was presented as a paper at South Atlantic Modern Language Association, Italian Section, Washington, D.C., November 1974; Chapter VIII at the Conference of the Southern Comparative Literature Association, University of Tennessee at Knoxville, February, 1975.

The separate publication or presentation as papers of these chapters accounts for any repetition of ideas. As separate essays it was necessary to reiterate on each occasion the general purpose and the results of the comparison between Donne and Petrarch as it defined the context of each specific study. It would not have been necessary to do so if the essays had appeared together as one integral work.

CONTENTS

I. "THE UNWANTED HEART"

Some of the more recent studies of John Donne's *Songs and Sonnets* focus on the central problem of his relationship to a Continental tradition of love poetry.[1] Most have attempted to show in what ways Donne followed or deviated from this tradition and what qualities in his treatment of love account for its seeming uniqueness. Donne is no longer viewed as a revolutionary innovator who rejected conventional love poetry in favor of a more realistic, personal approach, but instead he is seen as having adapted and brought to their logical fulfillment the traditions which he undoubtedly knew.

The emphasis on Donne's relationship to Continental love poetry has taken two forms: one seeing him as a part of the contemporary Baroque-Mannerist movement, and one seeing him as a descendant of Petrarch, in which case his poems may be compared with the European parodists of Petrarch, or they may be directly compared with the poems of Petrarch himself. A comparative analysis of how Donne assimilated motifs and techniques which Petrarch also used shows that Donne's greatness as an innovator lies in his " imitation " of Petrarch, in his discovery of latent and undeveloped possibilities of treating love within the Petrarchan mode itself. Donne's poems reveal a conscious and pervasive awareness of the attitudes, conceits, and situations common to Petrarch's *Canzoniere*, but Petrarch was not for Donne as he was for others simply a repository of fashionable conceits and mannerisms; nor was he simply the object of satiric ridicule. In fact, when Donne's treatment of a motif, such as the unwanted heart, is compared directly with Petrarch's, Donne's version is revealed not as a mordant attack on Petrarch at all, but as a fresh interpretation of conventions by juxtaposing the excellencies of the ideal to the disenchantments of the real.

The nature of the love situation in Petrarch's *Canzoniere* is symbolized by the conceit of the " unwanted heart." The lover freely gives his heart to a lady who, unappreciative of his devoted gift, reciprocates with cruelty and coldness. It is a situation in which Petrarch's faith in and dependence on the lady have yielded him nothing but pain and sorrow. Yet he persists in his monogamous and submissive role. Since he is unable to control his emotional attachment, the lady has complete psychological superiority. He allows her to determine his happiness or sadness. Occasionally, the lady gives a sign of acceptance, but more often Petrarch is in a position of constant pleading or complaining. Realizing the futility of his devotion, he tries to retrieve his unwanted heart, but he is unable to convert his intellectual awareness into concrete action. For a time he may succeed in regaining his heart, only to give it back again; or he may delude himself into thinking he has retrieved it, only to find that it was with the lady all the while.

Petrarch's " Mira quel colle, o stanco mio cor vago "[2] offers an example of how he treats the motif of the unwanted heart.

> —Mira quel colle, o stanco mio cor vago:
> ivi lasciammo ier lei, ch'alcun tempo ebbe
> qualche cura di noi, et le ne 'ncrebbe,
> or vorria trar de li occhi nostri un lago.
>
> Torna tu in la', ch'io d'esser sol m'appago;
> tenta se forse anchor tempo sarebbe
> da scemar nostro duol, che 'nfin qui crebbe,
> o del mio mal participe et presago.
>
> —Or tu ch'ài posto te stesso in oblio
> et parli al cor pur come e' fusse or teco,
> miser, et pien di pensier' vani et sciocchi!
>
> ch'al dipartir dal tuo sommo desio
> tu te n'andasti, e' si rimase seco,
> et si nascose dentro a' suoi belli occhi.

Petrarch leaves Laura after a misunderstanding. The next day, as he stands at the foot of the hill where Laura lives, he asks his heart, which he thinks he took back with him, to return to Laura to pacify their disagreement. But as he speaks to his heart, a voice answers saying that he only fooled himself into thinking he had retrieved his heart, for it still remains with her. In calling his heart " stanco mio cor vago... del mio mal participe et presago " Petrarch reveals his full self-knowledge about the hopelessness of his situation. The conceit of the unwanted heart is a projection of the lover himself, for just as he vainly persists in his love, he paradoxically allows his heart to abide with the lady despite her mistreatment and neglect. The heart separated from the lover and unwanted by the lady dramatizes how with complete resignation he has victimized himself to an unreciprocated love.

Some of Donne's *Songs* expand the basic characteristics of the Petrarchan motif of the unwanted heart. One or two of his poems recreate the situation with little modification, while several more extend its implications far beyond the original form to prove the deeper implications as they apply to practical experience. " The Blossom " and " The Broken Heart " demonstrate his imitation and variation of the Petrarchan motif of the unwanted heart by showing how it acts as a basis for a continuing exploration into its meaning. The situation is extended from the removed, confined, and meditative world of Petrarchan love into the accessible and active world of men, where it is carried out to its logical conclusion.

" The Blossom " is an apparent dialogue between the lover and his heart, which he compares to a flower, neglected and mistreated by a cold, unresponsive lady.[3]

THE BLOSSOM

Little thinkst thou, poore flower,
    Whom I' have watch'd sixe or seaven dayes,
And seene thy birth, and seene what every houre
Gave to the growth, thee to this height to raise,
And now dost laugh and triumph on this bough,
    Little think'st thou
That it will freeze anon, and that I shall
To morrow finde thee falne, or not at all.

    Little think'st thou poore heart
    That labour'st yet to nestle thee,
And think'st by hovering here to get a part

In a forbidden or forbidding tree,
And hop'st her stiffenesse by long siege to bow:
            Little think'st thou,
That thou to morrow, ere that Sunne doth wake,
Must with this Sunne, and mee a journey take.

        But thou which lov'st to bee
            Subtile to plague thy selfe, wilt say,
Alas, if you must goe, what's that to mee?
Here lyes my businesse, and here I will stay:
You goe to friends, whose love and meanes present
            Various content
To your eyes, eares, and tongue, and every part.
If then your body goe, what need you a heart?

        Well, then, stay here; but know,
            When thou hast stayd and done thy most;
A naked thinking heart, that makes no show,
Is to a woman, but a kinde of Ghost;
How shall shee know my heart; or having none,
            Know thee for one?
Practise may make her know some other part,
But take my word, shee doth not know a heart.

        Meet mee at London, then,
            Twenty dayes hence, and thou shalt see
Mee fresher, and more fat, by being with men,
Then if I had staid still with her and thee.
For Gods sake, if you can, be you so too:
            I would give you
There, to another friend, whom wee shall finde
As glad to have my body, as my minde.[4]

With his commonsense approach, the lover tries to warn his heart about the deadening effects of the lady's cold indifference, but the heart, having a mind of its own, replies by reaffirming its continued devotion to the lady and its explicit rejection of the mundane world. But the lover's argument, which takes up the first two and the last two stanzas, vitiates the effectiveness of the heart's one stanza defense. In addressing his heart in the first stanza, the speaker compares its existence to that of a delicate flower susceptible to the deadening chill of early spring. The flower analogy should convince his heart to abandon the lady to take a trip with him. He tries to persuade the heart

by saying that, like the flower, it is ignorant of the consequences
that await if it persists with no hope of acceptance:

> Little think'st thou, poore, flower,...
> Little think'st thou
> That it will freeze anon...

Moreover, the flower provides the speaker with an apt comparison, for it lends itself well to his habit of using conventional
images throughout the poem to characterize the heart's Petrarchan devotion, as, for example, his implied assertion that the
flower-heart will " freeze " because it is not warmed by the
Sun's-lady's reciprocated warmth.

In stanza two the Petrarchan conceits become more overt
and numerous, as the speaker further defines the situation of
the unwanted heart. The heart insists on " hovering... In a
forbidden or forbidding tree." Gardner's note on the line acknowledges that, " This is a Petrarchan situation where the
mistress who denies is married." [5] It is further emphasized by
the use of war imagery in the next line to refer to the lady's
chastity, " And hop'st her stiffenesse by long siege to bow."
The line recalls Petrarch's similar use of war imagery in " Mille
fiate, o dolce mia guerrera," where he vainly resorts to the
gift of his heart as a way of concluding peace with his warring
lady, only to have it totally and unconditionally rejected:

> Mille fiate, o dolce mia guerrera,
> per aver co' begli occhi vostri pace,
> v'aggio proferto il cor; m'a voi non piace
> mirar si' basso colla mente altera.
>
> -XXI

The speaker's use of the Petrarchan term " Sunne " to refer to
the lady in line 15 of " The Blossom " further stresses the
conventional nature of the love.

Stanza three presents the heart's defense, but it is not a
direct answer from the heart. Instead, the speaker imagines
what the heart might respond and projects it as a quote. He
believes that the focus of the heart's defense will center on its
dispraise of the mundane, physical world. He imagines that

the heart would answer, " You goe to friends, whose love and meanes present / Various content / To your eyes, eares, and tongue, and every world." The heart's defense is that its " businesse " lay not in the concerns of the body, implying the spiritual nature of its involvement. The heart says that since the speaker will concern himself on his trip with the gratification of his body's desires, then he has no need for the heart to go with him.

The lover retorts in stanza four that despite all its effort to make the lady accept the heart, " A naked thinking heart, that makes no show, / Is to a woman, but a kinde of Ghost." The contrast is between the words " thinking," implying meditation but no action, and " show," suggesting action.[6] The speaker continues his habit of using analogies by saying that in the lady's eyes " a naked thinking heart," one which fails to change contemplation into action, is like a " Ghost " to the lady. The lines suggest that the heart is unwanted by the lady because of its inaction. The " naked thinking heart " is a projection or extension of the contemplative Petrarchan lover, monogamous, idealistic, and loyal, but whose inaction is as useless to the lady as a " Ghost." But in the last four lines of the stanza we discover the real reason for the speaker's warning to the heart. The lady herself would not recognize his heart, because she has none of her own, alluding to the Petrarchan accusation of the " heartless " lady. More than this, however, the lady would not recognize his heart because she has not had practice in doing so, as she has had practice in recognizing other parts of the body. These mordant lines suggest that the lady's inability to know and accept the heart results from her infidelity and sensuality. The lines also qualify the idealized Petrarchan terms used in stanza two, 11. 11-15, to describe the lady. Thus, the speaker supplements the Petrarchan claim of the heartless lady with his more realistic awareness of the inconstant nature of women as he knows it, in an attempt to explain to the heart why it is unwanted.

The final stanza is a resolve on the speaker's part to proceed on his trip despite the heart's refusal. In twenty days when he returns to the city after being away in the company

of men, the heart will see him " fresher, and more fat... / Then
if I had staid still with her and thee " —a cynical comment
on the self-destructive effect of the physical relationship with
his lady. The lines also qualify the heart's accusation that the
lover is merely interested in the physical needs of his body, for
if this were true he would not refer to them in such derogatory
terms. The lover, aware of his weakness, decides to do something
about it. More importantly, the lines imply that the reward
the speaker seeks is more than just physical satisfaction, for
he admits that he has already received it and not found it
enough. What the speaker seeks, then, is her heart, that is,
her love. It is in this sense that she fits the Petrarchan idea of
the heartless lady, for in refusing him her heart she has refused
her love. The stanza is also an exhortation to the heart to go
with him, in which case he would see to it that the heart is
given " to another friend, whom we shall find / As glad to
have my body, as my minde." Implying the need for balance in
a love relationship, he expresses the hope of finding a more
appreciative recipient for this heart.

If we consider Donne's treatment of the motif of the
unwanted heart in the light of Petrarch's " Mira quel colle,"
for example, certain similarities and differences are evident.
Both poems offer two points of view—the romantic and the
realistic. The realistic side of the lover's character tries to warn
the romantic about the uselessness of an unqualified devotion
to a rejecting lady. Although both lovers realize intellectually
that unrewarded love is self-destructive and foolish, it is Donne's
speaker who operatively vows to correct the situation. Petrarch
remains crippled and confined in his circle of solitude and
contemplation. In Petrarch's sonnet we find only an awareness
of a hopeless love, while in Donne this awareness is transformed
into action. The lover has decided to abandon the lady and he
tries to convince his heart to do so. Petrarch has fooled himself into thinking his heart left with him.

Another difference is that Donne's speaker is not content
to accept the Petrarchan notion that the lady should spurn his
heart without probing the reasons for such a rejection. Such
probing leads him to conclude that the conventional description

of the Petrarchan lady as heartless by nature is only part of
the reason; the other, her possible infidelity and sensuality,
recognizes a more realistic explanation based on the lessons of
experience. Petrarch accepts the rejection without questioning
the reasons. Yet in both poems the speakers love the lady, but
for Petrarch it is an unqualified love, while for Donne it is
a conditional love open to change as dictated by experience.
He is unwilling to accept Petrarchan love as literally true until
he tests its applicability to a specific situation. He does not
discredit the idea of the " naked thinking heart " in and of
itself, for we suspect that if the lady were not heartless and
inconstant, it would have his full acceptance. After all, the heart
is in fact a projection of an essential part of his own being and
what the heart believes as true is partially what he believes.
But it is because the speaker finds that the kind of love symbolized by the " naked thinking heart " is inapplicable to *every*
situation that he vows to leave the lady. Significantly, the last
lines of the poem proffer the hope for a more fruitful relationship in the future, one balancing the demands of the body with
those of the mind. Thus, " The Blossom " is not merely a lover's
complaint of the lady's cold indifference to his physical desire,
nor is it a repetition of the Petrarchan ideal of the devoted and
monogamous heart; rather it is a realistic and sensible probing
into the implications of the Petrarchan idealized conceit as it
applies to a practical situation.

"The Broken Heart " offers another example of how Donne
varies the situation of the unwanted heart.

THE BROKEN HEART

He is starke mad, who ever sayes,
  That he hath beene in love an houre,
Yet not that love so soone decayes,
  But that it can tenne in lesse space devour;
Who will beleeve mee, if I sweare
That I have had the plague a yeare?
    Who would not laugh at mee, if I should say,
    I saw a flaske of powder burne a day?

Ah, what a trifle is a heart,
    If once into loves hands it come!

All other griefes allow a part
　　To other griefes, and aske themselves but some;
They come to us, but as Love draws,
Hee swallows us, and never chawes:
　　By him, as by chain-shot, whole rankes doe dye,
　　He is the tyran Pike, our hearts the Frye.

If t'were not so, what did become
　　Of my heart, when I first saw thee?
I brought a heart into the roome,
　　But from the roome, I carried none with mee:
If it had gone to thee, I know
Mine would have taught thine heart to show
　　More pitty unto mee: but Love, alas,
　　At one first blow did shiver it as glasse.

Yet nothing can to nothing fall,
　　Nor any place be empty quite,
Therefore I thinke my breast hath all
　　Those peeces still, though they be not unite;
And now as broken glasses show
A hundred lesser faces, so
　　My ragges of heart can like, wish, and adore,
　　But after one such love, can love no more.

The speaker in this poem seems at first to be renouncing the
ideal world of Petrarchan love as projected through its conceits. He says that it is unrealistic to describe himself or his
feelings in terms of the stereotyped Petrarchan lover, who burns
and freezes with love [7] and who loses his heart to an unappreciative mistress. But once he tells his little story about the
heart and how it was struck with Love's arrows, we realize
that his desire to change the words which describe his situation
does not alter his essential predicament.

Donne's poem describes how the lover fell in love at first
sight. Its form is that of the Petrarchan *innamoramento* poem,
in which Petrarch recounts the details of his falling in love—a
form occurring frequently in the *Canzoniere*, as attested by sonnets II, LXV, CXXXII, CXXXIV, CCXXVIII. For example, in
sonnet II Petrarch recounts how Love attacked him, wounding
him with the arrow of monogamous devotion to Laura. The
form here emphasizes the suddenness of the attack, the helpless-
ness of the lover, and the unrelenting and tyrannical nature of

Love's power. In sonnet LXV he describes how through the wound which Love inflicted on his heart he has become Love's powerless subject, while in sonnet CCXXVIII he recalls how Love deftly opened his left side and planted " a green laurel " in the middle of his heart. Sonnets CXXXII and CXXXIV present the other characteristic typical of the *innamoramento* form— that of the lover's description of his paradoxical physical symptoms resulting from Love's wound. The symptoms are expressed as antithetical feelings, or, as Petrarch calls them, " Warring winds " (" contrari venti ").

E tremo a mezza state, ardendo il verno

-CXXXII

Et ardo, et son un ghiaccio.

-CXXXIV

The conceits are the lover's way of dramatizing and projecting the intensity of his passion.

The opening stanza of " The Broken Heart," then, is an apparent rejection of these Petrarchan conceits as inaccurate descriptions of the lover's real state. Moreover, the speaker refuses to accept the validity of the conceits as expressive modes because they are in conflict with a realistic conception of time. Donne's lover is saying that the conceits of the timeless, ideal Petrarchan world seem ridiculous when considered in the context of a real, time-ridden world of which he thinks he is a part. Words suggesting time or the effects of time in a real world are numerous in the stanza (*houre, decayes, devour, yeare, day*). The speaker underscores the impossibility of continued passion over an extended period of time, a probable derogation of Petrarch who pines away for twenty years or more.[8] The speaker points out the difference between real time in his active world of love and imagined time in the contemplative world of Petrarch's *Canzoniere*.

Yet, as the poem continues, his apparent mockery of Petrarchan claims undergoes a considerable modification. Although the first stanza professes to negate the validity of Petrarchan love, it is instead an indirect affirmation that the speaker *is* in love. In fact, by supplementing the conceits of the ideal Petrarchan world of love with a realistic awareness of the demands of time in a real world, he has emphasized even more the intensity of his love, for he is affirming the sentiments of the conceits by saying they are too strong to survive for an extended time. He also implies that his love is more sincere than that of a lover like Petrarch, who, if he truly felt the sentiments the conceits suggests, could not have survived so long. Thus, it is not the idea of Petrarchan love that he is rejecting, but rather the accuracy of its language as applied to a real love experience.

Stanza two presents a philosophical commentary on the absolute and universal tyranny of Love over man's heart. Such a commentary is typical of Petrarch, who recognizes that he is Love's powerless captive. Consider, for example, Petrarch's similar realization in LXV, among others:

> Lasso, che mal accorto fui da prima
> nel giorno ch'a ferir mi venne Amore,
> ch'a passo a passo e' poi fatto signore
> de la mia vita, et posto in su la cima.

From his specific situation Petrarch draws a universal lesson, which, as an insight or form of self-knowledge, helps him in turn to understand his own predicament. The speaker of " The Broken Heart " uses the explanation he gives himself in stanza two as a way of understanding what has happened to his heart:

> If 'twere not so, what did become
> Of my heart, when I first saw thee?

In stanza three we learn that what has happened to his heart is consistent with the fate of all Petrarchan hearts—it has been disdained by a pitiless lady. But the speaker works his own variation of this basic conceit. He initially thinks that his heart has left him to abide with the lady, but he muses if this were true then his loving heart would have taught hers how to love:

> If it had gone to thee, I know
> Mine would have taught thy heart to show
> More pitty unto me.

Since the lady does not love him, then he concludes in stanza four that his heart is still with him, but broken, not only by Love's mortal " first blow (which) did shiver it as glasse," but also by the lady's rejection. Although the pieces of his broken and unwanted heart reflect the faces of other women he could love with perhaps a more fruitful result, nevertheless, as a true Petrarchan lover he vows fidelity. The details of his predicament have reaffirmed the Petrarchan pose which the opening stanza seemed to negate. The ideal world suggested by the Petrarchan language and seemingly rejected by the lover as inconsistent with reality is now affirmed by the nature of the love experience he has unwittingly revealed. The language could be changed, but the essence of the situation would remain the same. He is a Petrarchan lover who suffers from an unwanted, and in this case, a broken heart. The Petrarchan ideal world as projected through its conceits partakes of the real world, regardless of the words.

Donne's adaptation of the motif of the unwanted heart in " The Blossom " and " The Broken Heart " shows that he could express himself creatively within the conventional limits of Petrarchanism. As he probes the significance of what it means to be in love, Donne often includes rather than rejects the Petrarchan world of idealized passion and ritualistic adoration. He extends the implications of its meaning and practical application by re-evaluating the Petrarchan ideal in terms of how the romantic vision of things as he would like them to be modifies his realistic awareness of the world's demands. Donne's relationship to Petrarch is more complex than either Petrarchist imitator or revolutionary innovator will allow. The Petrarchists were often content to parody Petrarch's diction and refine his conceits, but they were rarely successful in catching his spirit. For them, the mechanics of Petrarchanism became ends in themselves. Donne neither imitates nor rejects Petrarchan conceits, language, or situations, but rather builds on their implications by probing how its code and idiom relate to experience. In carrying Petrarchan thought and expression a step further, he made an original contribution to the mode and, thus, can be rightly called as much an innovator as Petrarch was in his day.

II. DONNE'S 'PARODY'
OF THE PETRARCHAN LADY

The dominant characteristic of Petrarch's *Canzoniere* is constancy to the lady. His idealized notion of the lady nurtures his constancy despite the prospect of continued rejection. Petrarch builds the details of his exaltation of Laura on a scaffolding of fiction and personal myth. The imaginative terms used to define her birthplace, origin, and residence combined with her exceptional beauty and ennobling influence all contribute to creating Laura's apotheosized image. The place where she was born and lived is described as an arcadian paradise, as seen in the famous canzone " Chiare, fresche et dolci acque." Often he pictures her in the open air setting of grass, trees, and flowers—an earthly Eden.[1] Among the other phenomena of nature she is a spectacle of supreme perfection. Petrarch perpetuates Laura's mystic quality by conveying her origin through the use of astrological imagery. As " un spirto gentil di paradiso," her birth was accompanied by the appearance of favorable stars; in fact, she herself is a star on earth:

> Benigne stelle che compagne fersi
> al fortunato fiancho
> quando 'l bel parto giù nel mondo scorse!
> ch'e' stella in terra...   -XXIX

In sonnets IX and CCXIX he portrays her as a child of the whole universe and as a sun in her own right. Petrarch's praise of the lady's beauty mixes Neoplatonic idealization and religious analogy, as in sonnet CC. But sonnet CCXV offers the finest Petrarchan expression of Laura's infinite virtue, heavenly beauty, and incomprehensible but visible effect on the world:

> In nobil sangue vita humile et queta
> et in alto intellecto un puro core,
> frutto senile in sul giovenil fiore
> e 'n aspetto pensoso anima lieta

raccolto a 'n questa donna il suo pianeta,
   anzi 'l re de le stelle; e 'l vero honore,
   le degne lode, e 'l gran pregio, e 'l valore,
   ch' è da stanchar ogni divin poeta.
Amor s'è in lei con honestate aggiunto,
   con beltà naturale habito adorno,
   et un atto che parla con silentio;
et non so che nelli occhi, che 'n un punto
   po' far chiara la notte, oscuro il giorno,
   e 'l mel amaro, et adolcir l'assentio.

Although Laura represents the most perfect of human
women, to assume that Petrarch's attitude toward her is totally
one-sided neglects his ironic ambivalence, simplifies his textual
complexity, and miscalculates his clear-cut distinction from previous treatments of the lady figure.[2] Because his attitude is not
always idealizing, Laura's image prevails as an essentially human
one. On many occasions reality and cynicism intrude, effecting
a drastically humanized view. Moreover, Petrarch's vacillating
attitude toward her dictates a similarly inconsistent attitude
toward the ideal of constancy. When he idealizes her, he vows
his eternal devotion, as in sonnet CXLV, in which he swears
endless adoration. But when he detects her faults or weaknesses,
he ponders other alternatives to his present course, even though
he may not have the courage to actuate those alternatives. For
example, in sonnet XLV he condemns Laura for loving her own
image more than him. Observing her gazing admiringly at her
face in a mirror, Petrarch warns her of the irreversible consequences of vain self-love by recalling the mythological story of
Narcissus. But his warning is more of a threat which he already
imagines realized. Sonnet LX condemns Laura for not returning
his love, and Petrarch apologizes to all those who having faith in
his verse lost their way because they had placed hope in love.
A substitute symbol, the laurel tree, to whom the sonnet is
addressed, elegantly veils his subtle criticism, but his gallantry
cannot hide the fact that in reality he is cursing his lady's scorn
and deceit:

Né poeta ne colga mai, né Giove
   la privilegi; et al Sol venga in ira,
   tal che si secchi ogni sua foglia verde.

In sonnet LXXXII Petrarch is bitter in his rejection and unsuccessful in his search for a remedy to cure his diseased passion. He warns the lady that although in the past he endured her unreturned love, now he has grown to hate his submissive and frustrating role, and become weary of his constant but futile tears. As a way of punishing the lady, he desires to die and to be placed in a marble sepulcher, on which her name will be inscribed as the cause of his death for all future generations to see. In sonnet LXXXVII by his comparison of Laura to an archer, who deliberately draws his bow for a good shot, Petrarch reveals his condemnation of her cold and cruel flirting, which plays unmercifully with sincere human passion. Sonnet CLXXIV reiterates the same theme using much of the same imagery. The lady is compared to a savage, fiery star, who ruled the heavens at his birth and who destined his life for torment. He compares her to an archer, who wounded him with love and who cruelly toys with his painful wound. But despite his vivid description of her pitiless and destructive scorn, he vows, " che languir per lei / meglio è, che gioir d'altra." It is significant that the thought of inconstancy even crosses his mind, and we wonder at the strength of his vow in the light of the intensity of his suffering. In sonnet CLXXI his vow to love Laura eternally appears ironical in the context of Petrarch's criticism of her insufferable pride and cruelty.

Yet, despite all this, occasionally Laura softens her pose, eliciting subtle hints that the love was not totally unrequited. The opening lines of CXLIX suggest that with time Laura has relented in her severity and has conceded some favors to her lover. Her concessions have only whetted his appetite for more rewards:

> ché più m'arde 'l desio,
> quanto più la speranza m'assicura.

Sonnet CLXXII indicates that at one time the love relationship was reciprocal, but now the envy of profane people compels Laura to refuse his advances. Petrarch's severe admonition of Laura in sonnet LX seems motivated by the fact that at one time " i bei rami non m'ebber a sdegno." And again, his

philosophical observation on the inconstancy of a woman's will
in sonnet CLXXXIII is motivated by her apparent reciprocation
of his love for a time, but he fears she may return to her
previous severity.

In the Provençal and *dolce stil nuovo* tradition the lady
was the localization of the ideal, " an image that accommodated
the infirmities of secular life," and as such most of these poets
" did not go beyond this point to question the moral indispen-
sability of the figure they praise." [3] Petrarch's vision of the lady
is basically idealized, but often his drastically humanized and
critical portrayal, although veiled, suggests that he did not fully
accept this unrealistic view.[4] He presents a qualifying approach,
which John Donne and others would extend, of probing the
inadequacies of this ideal lady. Petrarch does not exalt his
lady to the point of denying her humanity, as many Provençal
poets do; yet he retains other characteristics of the courtly
system. For example, his poems create an imaginary world of
illusion and fiction in which the whole amorous experience is
falsified. Fantasy, dreams, imaginings, and meditation replace
the reality of action. The lover by replacing " the unattainable
lady with her manipulated image " creates a dream world of
"...surrogate experience free of all the risks and limitations of
real experience." The " theater of the animated image " provided
a temporary solace, or even fulfillment for the lover, who desires
a real encounter with the lady, but who lacks the courage to
face possible disappointment.[5] Despite intimations of the lady's
inadequacies, for Petrarch the self-contained, unqualified world
of illusion enflames and even perpetuates his monogamous constancy.

Critics have often claimed that one of Donne's original
contributions to the development of Petrarchan love poetry
was his realistic and cynical portrayal of women.[6] " Womans
Constancy " or " The Indifferent " are cited as dramatic proof
of Donne's disavowal of Petrarch's soft, musical cadences and
misguided, illusory praise of an idealized lady. There *are* notable
differences between the two treatments, and Donne's portrayal
is " original " in several distinctive ways, but not because he
is " cynical " (a term needing more specific definition) or because

he supposedly spurned the traditional image of the Petrarchan lady-figure. In fact, an analysis of Donne's method of adapting the Petrarchan ideals of woman and constancy undercuts the oversimplified view of innovative revolt, for it will reveal how Donne assimilated Petrarch to his own poetic needs and temperament.

In evaluating the extent of Donne's originality and independence, it is too facile to conclude that his poems are un-Petrarchan because they show mistrust, cynicism, or sarcasm toward women. " Cynicism " cannot be used as a comprehensive term to cover all kinds of gradations of feeling, and even Petrarch is not always idealizing in his portrayal. Moreover, we cannot assume that what the poetic persona says in the poems about women is always an indication of what Donne personally believed. The poet may use cynicism as a dramatic technique to present a fictionalized speaker in an ironic light.[7] Thus, to ignore the dramatic and ironic perspective is to misinterpret the source and object of Donne's cynicism in his treatment of women. Donne's cynical pose shows that he does not purely reject the Petrarchan ideals of woman and constancy, but instead, he varies or redefines them in the context of practical experience. He takes the eccentricities of the Petrarchan ideals and thoroughly applies them to a particular situation. The idealized Petrarchan attitude persists in his thought as an assumption underlying his explicit statement and functioning as a kind of implied standard of comparison. The " cynical " poem often explores the complexities of a point of view, usually extreme, to which the ideal seems opposed, doing so for the purpose of redefining the ideal in the context of an enlarged gamut of experience.

Although Petrarch is aware of his lady's weakness or faults, and although he may threaten inconstancy or revenge, his awareness remains essentially introspective and contemplative. Donne's speakers take the Petrarchan situation to its natural conclusion when placed in a realistic and active world. The women in the *Songs* represent a joining of the real with the ideal. The realism of Donne's portrayal resides not in any personal glimpses into the libertine psyche of " Jack " Donne, but in the speaker's attitude toward the lady, or in the situation in which we see her. The noted risque humor, cynicism, and sarcasm in his poems often operate as a mask for his implied juxtaposition of real and ideal in a dramatic situation, which demands an active response from the protagonists, not mere meditative imaginings. Cynicism can result from disappointment and disillusionment when an accepted and cherished ideal is disregarded. Donne's ruse of the cynical mask, perhaps one of his unique contributions to the evolvement of the Petrarchist tradition, should not be mistaken for a negation of the ideal. It is his original way of showing how the ideal partakes of reality, and how human nature, although aware of the ideal, refuses to exert the virtuous energy required to make the ideal possible and practical in the real world.

Petrarch, in contrast to Dante, regarded woman as a vessel capable of stimulating an ecstasy that could approximate a state of divine grace. However, the ecstasy or grace remained consummate within the vessel. There is no Platonic ladder or Beatrician ascent. Instead, Petrarch's highly personal feelings and statements about man's love and the nature of woman are effusive, intense, irreverent, and self-consumming.

As the drama of the *Canzoniere* unfolds, it is Petrarch's grief rather than Laura's virtues that are celebrated, especially in the sonnets after her death. Laura comes to symbolize the artistically unattainable. While Dante submits in the last lines of the *Paradiso* to the aposiopesic nature of art when confronted with a manifestation of the divine, Petrarch grieves for failing to commit incest with his own creation. Petrarch believed that Laura lived as long as his feelings lived and what immortality she had resulted from the immortal grief his art created. That the fictive Laura was a woman further represents Petrarch's doubt about lasting unions between men and women. He may imply that in this life we may be certain of our own feelings, but not another's. For immortality we may be certain of our own art, not our feelings.

Whereas Petrarch took the first steps toward humanizing Dante's totally spiritual conception of women, Donne extended Petrarch's partially humanized view into an even more down-to-earth situation. Just as Petrarch did not reject Dante's vision, but built on it, so, too, Donne with Petrarch. As a true innovator, Donne interpreted the Petrarchan ideal according to his own poetic vision.

" Song: Goe and catche a falling starre " offers an example of how Donne varies the Petrarchan motif of the ideal lady who elicits her lover's constancy. It demonstrates how Donne redefines the motif in the light of practical experience, and how the attitude toward constancy is directly related to whether the lover idealizes the lady or not. The poem has often been cited as an example of Donne's attack on the Petrarchan practice of deifying the lady.[8] But the romantic ideal abides in the poem more than commonly thought.

In the first two stanzas the speaker lists a series of impossibilities, strange or perverse things, all drawn from an imaginary world of romance. Falling stars, mandrakes, mermaids, a human nature devoid of envy and dishonesty are all characteristic of a " golden world," in which the " woman true and faire " would not be uncommon. The poem is a variation of two specific kinds of sonnets appearing frequently in the *Canzoniere*. In the first kind, Petrarch compares his lady's virtue (chastity and constancy are equivalent to Donne's " true ") and beauty (" faire ") to the phenomenal in the world of reality. For example, in sonnet CLXXXV he idealizes Laura's beauty by comparing it to the exquisite beauty and rare qualities of the phoenix. He parallels her appearance and dress to that of the mythical bird purported to have risen from its own ashes. Or again, in sonnet CCX he says that were one to travel to the four corners of the earth, he could find " né 'n ciel né 'n terra, è più d'una fenice." In sonnet CLXXXVI he says that his lady's beauty and virtue are of such an exceptional kind that only the great poets of antiquity, Homer and Virgil, could have had the skill to describe it. Sonnet CCXIII answers those who say that he must be mad to praise Laura so much, by explaining that the strange " magicians " responsible for his illness are all her rare graces: her blond hair, her humility and chastity, her singing voice, heavenly gait, penetrating speech, and reasonable mind.

In the second kind of sonnet, the quest sonnet, Petrarch uses an extended conceit to compare his endless search in other women for his lady's " la disiata vostra forma vera " (XVI). He says that his quest is like the religious pilgrimage of an old man, who goes to Rome to see the image of Christ. Absent from Laura, he seeks to find in other women a trace or resemblance of the beauty and virtue which Laura possesses, but his quest is unsuccessful, for her qualities are unique.

The speaker of Donne's poem in the first stanza affirms the Petrarchan assertion that the true and fair lady belongs to a world of magnificent wonders and impossibilities. Ironically, the lover is unknowingly swearing his fidelity to an ideal whose meaning has become lost in the real world. In the second and third stanzas he resorts to the Petrarchan quest imagery with some variation. Petrarch's old pilgrim is suggested in Donne's lines:

> Ride ten thousand daies and nights,
>   Till age snow white haires on thee,
> . . . .
> If thou findst one, let mee know,
>   Such a Pilgrimage were sweet.

The poem is, in fact, an expression of the lover's veiled quest for the lost ideal, which in Petrarch's imaginary and introspective world is a reality. For after all, in the Petrarchan world of love impossibilities and miracles are commonplace, and the lady herself is the most dramatic expression of this fact. Donne's speaker does not deny that in the golden world the ideal is possible, and his fascination with this idea is heightened by his use of the Petrarchan quest image.

The tension in stanza three results from the juxtaposition of the ideal world of romantic Petrarchan love to a real world of actuality. The cynical comment on the inutility of writing a love letter to the lady suggests that since experience shows that the ideal lady is not possible, then constancy is of little significance also. Yet we recall that the speaker's cynicism results from his very idealism. He has attempted to extend his high principles to a real world, and cynicism results because he expected far more than he disappointingly received. But it is not the ideal that is at fault. His last lines suggest that earthly women refuse to live up to the ideal, implying that if things were different, he would not be cynical. Our evaluation of the speaker's pose is qualified by the unwitting revelation that he is a cynic who although he surfacely denounces women, he secretly wishes he could find one who is both true and fair.

In evaluating Donne's " cynical " poems it is revealing to determine the relationship of his version to the Petrarchan original. Donne's rendition is not simply an iconoclastic parody, for there is no outright rejection of Petrarchan absolutes. Rather they function as a basis for further commentary. Often the cynical poems reflect the dual awareness of the lyrical love poet, who recognizes the fruitful rewards that deceptive love can bring.[9] Moreover, the satirical statements in this poem are an expression of an extreme or pessimistic view, not to be taken entirely seriously. The speaker is not a spokesman for the author's views, nor does he directly reflect what the author believes.[10] Somewhere underneath all the cynicism and pessimism, the satiric writer secretly entertains an ideal vision whose survival is threatened or which is dead already.[11] Therefore, an analysis of Donne's content and parodic devices in relation to the Petrarchan ideal supports a qualified view of his realism and cynicism.

" Womans Constancy " demonstrates how the cynical pose veils the speaker's secret affiliation with the Petrarchan ideal. He seems to agree with his lady in his call for promiscuity, but the implications of his language expose his true beliefs about love. He assumes the pretended cynical role that constancy is as insignificant to him as it is to the lady, who he detects is tiring of the affair. He suspects her infidelity, and he imagines the excuses she will conjure as a way of ending it. Although his mistress' speech is intended as a reasonable and unemotional method of ending the affair, the language is subtly pregnant with terms and images—the indissoluble vow, oath, and contract—drawn from a Petrarchan world in which love is eternally constant and its stipulations are absolute. The list of possible excuses she will offer are perversions or negations of some ideal

value normally assumed in Petrarchan love. Thus, the paradox
of an unfaithful lady misapplying the language of faithful love
to justify her inconstancy is compounded because the lady's
justification is spoken by a lover who casually agrees with her
inconstancy, yet secretly desires it otherwise.

The lover's call for promiscuity is undermined by the legal
and religious imagery. If he were really as unconcerned as he
pretends, he would have no need to voice hypothetical excuses
and rationalizations. His cynicism is punctured by the inadver-
tent implications of his language. He is revealed as a disillusioned
idealist who assumes the cynical pose in order not to look
ridiculous when and if his lady ever does betray him, but he
is unable to hide his viewing this affair as an " image " of
what a true love relationship should be. Having lost faith in
the ability of this specific woman to be constant, he prepares
himself for her act of betrayal. As a proud man, he pretends
to be of the same mind as the lady, so that the " hurt won't
show." The insulting joke at the end of the poem—that he
will be as glad to be rid of her as she is of him—is directed
not at the ideal of constancy, but at the woman herself, who
he has imagined will abusively distort the language of love for
her own ends. She epitomizes human inadequacy and folly
failing before the prescribed demands of the ideal. The personal
insult discloses that his scorn is directed against human error,
and not at the ideal. Inwardly he nurtures the ideal conception
of the constant lovers, and he implicitly uses it as a standard
of comparison to judge his present situation. His disillusionment issues from the tacit comparison of real and ideal, for
the ideal lady would respect vows and oaths; she would not
change, and her love would not even end with death. But the
opening line of the poem, " Now that thou hast loved me one
whole day," by its emphasis on time, marks the relationship
as a decaying one; her " constancy " barely endures one whole
day. In an insecure and untrue love, time imposes a limiting
effect, while in the world of true love, hours, days, months and
years have no appreciable effect—time is eternal.

Donne's poem is a variation of Petrarch's sonnet CLXXXIII,
in which he tries to prepare himself for eventual rejection by

imagining what will be his fate if his lady leaves him. The
sonnet elegantly suggests that Laura had at one time reciprocated
his love, for he has enjoyed her words, smiles, and looks.
Petrarch's fears of her possible change in behavior are not
unfounded, he tells us, since, " questo temer d'antiche prove
è nato." He makes a gallant attempt to excuse Laura from his
fears, but he cannot help but notice her change (" ... veggio
cangiata sua figura "). His reluctant acknowledgment of her
volatility confirms his cynical but resigned conclusion about
woman's inability to persevere in love, and it seems also to
paraphrase what Donne's speaker knows about the failure and
incredibility of women:

> Femina è cosa mobil per natura:
> ond'io so ben ch'un amoroso stato
> in cor di donna picciol tempo dura.

Although Petrarch perceives the fluctuating nature of wom-
en, his manner seems naive and helpless when compared to
Donne's speaker. Petrarch can do nothing but lament his fate.
Donne's lover seems to possess a strong emotional superiority
absent in Petrarch. The situation and the conclusion of " Womans Constancy " are very much like that of sonnet CLXXXIII,
but Donne's speaker controls and dominates while Petrarch
secedes. Unlike Petrarch, who pitifully begs his lady not to
leave him, Donne's speaker tries to convince her he doesn't care.
But not because he loves her less. Perhaps his is a much
sounder method for keeping his lady. That a poem such as
" Womans Constancy " seems to advocate sexual promiscuity
cannot be cited as a proof of Donne's rejection of the Petrarchan ideal.

The speaker of " Communitie " bases his seemingly logical
argument for promiscuity on woman's moral neutrality, but he
reasons from a faulty equivocation of moral and ontological
good. He authenticates his cynicism with a rational basis, using
logic to shield his fundamentally hedonistic nature. The perspective by which to view " Communitie " is different from that of
" Song " or of " Womans Constancy." There speakers say one
thing, but secretly affiliate themselves with another way of

thinking. On the surface they seem to disavow the Petrarchan
ideal of woman and constancy, while underneath they wish it
were so. Here, and in the poem " Confined Love," speakers are
making sincere attempts to demolish the idea that woman is
pure and ennobling, but their efforts, although seemingly accurate philosophical justifications, are undercut by fallacious reasoning. Thus the speakers achieve the opposite result, of rein-
forcing what they are attempting to disprove. The poems are
examples of how Donne uses an accepted Petrarchan ideal as a
springboard for his own witty exploration of its significance.
This approach to Petrarch is unique in that he does not directly
accept the ideal by creating a pure imitation of the original, nor
does he simply reject the ideal by attacking its value. He instead
presents a speaker who seems to do one while actually doing
the other.

It was common for Neoplatonists, as in Book IV of Casti-
glione's *Il Cortegiano*, to use high-sounding philosophical arguments to justify their notions of the ennobling nature of women.
The speaker of " Communitie " parodies this practice by using
similarly high-sounding arguments to justify his plea for promiscuity, but the result is far from a logical proof of his position.
The form of his statements gives their fallacious content a
philosophical aura. Immoral and irrational behavior cannot be
legitimized by the surface form in which the words appear. The
shallow thought is exposed for what it is. The careful reader
finds himself asking, " Is what he recommends about how men
should treat women actually advisable? Can we accept his call
for 'communitie,' knowing how erroneous the reasoning is
behind the call? " The speaker who seems so intent on demol-
ishing the Petrarchan ideal by using the same methods as his
opponents fails miserably to prove his argument. Thus, Donne
has created a speaker whom he allows to abuse logic in order
to show that the speaker's argument against the Neoplatonic-
Petrarchan view of women is invalid.

" The Indifferent " offers another example of varying the
Petrarchan motif of constancy through the use of the cynical
mask. The poem has been traditionally viewed as " a spoofing
of the Petrarchan stereotypes " by the inversion of the conven-

tional pose of the Petrarchan lover. Hunt claims that the inversion takes the form of a " lover who regards constancy as a ' vice ' and promiscuity as the path of virtue and good sense, who sees love simply as lust, and who views women unromantically, as creatures who are normally as promiscuous as he is." Thus, the lover, by inverting the cherished values and literary effect of the conventional love poem, has " turned Petrarchanism upside down." [12]

There are indications in the poem, however, that this is an oversimplification of Donne's method. His treatment of the Petrarchan materials needs reevaluation in the light of his use of parodic and satiric devices traditionally thought to be directed against Petrarchan ideals. Often Donne appears on the surface to be ridiculing the Petrarchan ideals, but sometimes beneath the apparent cynicism abides the speaker's nostalgic and wistful desire for a return to the Petrarchan absolutes. In " The Indifferent " the argument for promiscuity seems to deny the Petrarchan ideal of constancy, but it is subtly undermined at crucial points by the ambiguous implications of the speaker's language and by his insight into feminine motives.

In the first stanza he seems to dispell the idea that he can love only that kind of woman commonly described in Petrarch's love sequence as a " blond ideal," and in the second stanza he seems especially critical of Petrarchan love's next most cherished ideal, constancy, which some women are attempting to reestablish. But the speaker begins to give himself away when he asks why they have changed from the traditional infidelity which their mothers followed. He designates their desire for constancy as a " vice," but at the same time he calls woman's customary dedication to infidelity in previous times as " old vice." The speaker's true position and attitude on constancy are further revealed by his question, " Or doth a fear, that men are true, torment you? " The question is used as a possible explanation for the ladies' change from infidelity to fidelity, although implicitly carrying with it a grain of truth. The question also carries the particular tone of a disillusioned idealist, who tries to adjust to a repugnant external reality by pretending to be an advocate of that very reality. The speaker appears to be emotionally uncommitted, but this is only self-defensive. His true attitude—that fidelity is still an important value to him—filters through the apparent denotation of his words. Perhaps realizing the implications of his questions, he quickly tries to cover up with, " Oh we are not, be not you so," but the retort is weak in the face of such forceful words as " fear," " true," and " torment " in the preceding question. Moreover, the speaker's question and answer coupled with his catalogue of different types of women at the beginning, suggest that he is not really convinced that women want to reestablish constancy at all, or if they do their motives are questionable. The impression that he realizes they want to use feigned fidelity as a way of dominating and possessing the lover completely is implied in the lines:

> Rob mee, but binde me not, and let me goe.
> Must I who came to travaile thorow you,
> Grow your fixt subject, because you are true?

It would seem that the ladies want constancy only to apply to the lover, while they are free to act as they please. In addition, the variety and abundance of women he lists as possible objects of his love renders questionable the probability that all of these different types could sincerely desire or adhere to the virtue of fidelity. Moreover, the qualities he cites as the distinguishing traits of each type do not create an idealized picture of woman, which in turn would support their supposed desire to reestablish constancy. The rhetorical questions in stanza two emphasize the speaker's doubt of their sincerity. The answers naturally expected or imagined, granting that the ladies *do* want constancy, are not the ones we will receive if they were to answer honestly out of the man's hearing. In other words, the lady secretly favors infidelity and probably is unfaithful, but in order to maintain a position of superiority over the man, the lady *says* she wants constancy. The speaker, on the other hand, truly favors fidelity, but he tries to give the impression that he desires promiscuity. Thus, it is really the man who maintains the upper hand (or at least tries to) in this situation, since he hides his own feelings while being aware of the lady's real and feigned attitude. He seemingly opposes her pretended desire (a return to constancy), while he is conscious of the selfish reason why she wants to reestablish constancy as a law of love.

As with many of Donne's poems, " The Indifferent " is best read within the context of a broader dramatic and rhetorical situation, which we must supply in order to understand the significance of the poem's statements. The speaker makes assertions which we cannot accept at face value, and we must scrutinize his words for indications of the true reality behind them. The lover seems to be using a conventional form to advocate unconventional behavior, but ironically he is not really advocating it at all. He assumes poses which hide his true beliefs and value in order to protect himself. And, what of the lady herself? What is her true nature? What are her true beliefs and motives? Is she really advocating fidelity as a value in and of itself, or does she want to use it as a weapon against the lover?

That the poem should be viewed within the context of a dramatic situation is strengthened by the break between stanzas two and three. Stanzas one and two are like a dramatic monologue suddenly thrown into perspective by the speaker's acknowledgment of his ranting and raving. Herbert uses the technique at the end of " The Collar " when he interrupts his speaker's " raving " against the divine claims of duty by changing the form of his statements from dramatic to narrative, " but as I rav'd and grew more fierce and wilde / At every word..." Donne uses the same technique at the beginning of stanza three, " Venus heard me sigh this song...," with a narrative commentary on the dramatic utterance in the previous stanzas. His use of the word " sigh "—a common word in Petrarchan laments—to describe the manner of his delivery is an ironic revelation of his true character. We suddenly realize that he is a disheartened Petrarchan lover who condemns women out of fear that he will never find a faithful woman to love him. He introduces a third character, Venus, into the little drama, just as Herbert introduces God as a speaking character at the end of his poem. Venus' role is to offer a judgment and solution to the question of fidelity versus infidelity, but her final words only strengthen the ambiguity of the lady's motives and the inutility of the speaker's argument for promiscuity. After her examination of the world's lover, she finds that only two or three women have become " heretics " in her religion of unfaithful love by wishing " to establish dangerous constancy." Obviously, they should have no appreciable effect on the behavior of the others. Thus, the speaker really has nothing to worry about, since constancy is far from becoming the general rule. Venus' role in the poem operates as a satiric device to highlight the instability and deceptiveness of human nature. She is true to the dictates of burlesque parody in which " ... supernatural figures are made human, all too human, talk coarsely, behave ridiculously, act ineffectively or absurdly. "[13] She is introduced by the speaker to give validity to his apparent argument for infidelity, but the intended purpose backfires. All she does is to emphasize even more the misuse of valuable ideals, this time by the gods themselves. Not even the gods can authenticate the value of constancy. If there is cynicism in " The Indifferent," it is directed not at the Petrarchan ideals of the ennobling woman or constancy, but at the human abuse or perversion of the ideal for selfish motives.

" The Indifferent " shows how Donne's witty and inventive approach presents the Petrarchan ideals in a new way. The poem does not simply parody Petrarchan ideals for the explicit intention of disparaging their value so that we admire them a little less than before. Instead we are repelled by the kind of speaker who might advocate indiscriminate promiscuity or the kind of woman who would use feigned fidelity as a whiplash to dominate her lover. It may even be that Donne is satirizing Petrarch's imitators who copied form but failed to capture his spirit. The poem's satiric attack is directed at the correction of human folly, and its ironic tension results from the ambivalent poses, motivations, and language of the participants. These Donne implicitly juxtaposes to the challenges, demands, and admitted limitations of Petrarchan ideal love—an inescapable basis for comparison.

III. AMOROUS ABBERRATIONS

Petrarch's amorous imagination allows him to idealize his love and his lady in the face of an unfulfilling reality. It allows him to persist in the role of constant devotion despite the frustration of actual experience, and it promotes a vision of the lady as an ennobling influence on the lover. He is uplifted by what he imagines as the virtuous effects of his love for Laura, whose beauty inspires all loving meditation and sometimes moves Petrarch to raise his thoughts to God (XIII). Petrarch portrays these virtuous effects in different ways. The lady is responsible for the return of good weather, as seen in sonnets XLII and XLIII, which describe how the flowers awake, malignant stars disappear, and a good sailing breeze arises when she returns after a long absence. She renews his life with each salute, and she inspires his faltering intellect. Her sight is divine food for his mind (CXCIII), causing him to forget every other earthly joy.[1]

Yet, concomitant with this strain of idealized, virtuous love is Petrarch's awareness that earthly love yields many evil effects. There is an explicit awareness throughout the *Canzoniere* that human love is often a vain, deceptive lie, promising the lover an earthly paradise, but yielding only the bitter fruits of pain and frustration. The first sonnet in the sequence presents a condemnation of the deceptions of human love. The sonnet is a prologue to the work, probably written in Petrarch's last years, but which he desired to put at the beginning of the *Canzoniere* in order to guide his readers on the moral significance of his love fiction. As a typical medieval introduction, it announces the argument of the book, and expresses regret for the inadequacy of the poet's skill. Recognizing the fragmentary nature of his sonnet collection, Petrarch acknowledges that the only unity he can give his work is that personal unity

of a lover repentant for his youthful error. He does not renounce writing about his love experiences because he hopes
other lovers will profit from the final lesson his profane love
taught him.

The sonnet addresses all those who have heard the sound
of his love sighs vocalized in scattered rhymes. He laments
that although in his youth he nourished his heart with these
love sighs, now as an experienced and wiser man he repents
his error, and he begs mercy and forgiveness from God for
the shame he has brought upon himself. He calls his experience
with love " 'il mio primo giovenile errore," a judgment carrying
Christian overtones, but which is a natural conclusion to any
grief-ridden, joyless love. He realizes the vanity of his hopes and
pains, for they did not render any of that terrestrial beatitude
promised by his love ideal. The only result of so much pain is
the shame of becoming a popular legend, a piece of tavern
gossip. He now repents in the discovery " che quanto piace al
mondo è breve sogno." Human love promises only an illusory
paradise, where the fruits of emptiness, affliction, and shame
flourish. As a microcosm of the whole *Canzoniere*, the sonnet
reflects the work's total movement away from the deceiving,
vain love for an earthly ideal to Petrarch's recognition of his
error, and his final attempt to substitute the Creator for the
creature. Despite the vacillation, doubt, contradiction, and
conflicting emotions characteristic of Petrarch's amorous contemplation and his poetic expression of his love, the work
nevertheless moves, if somewhat discursively, to a kind of
transcendence of human love.

Donne's *Songs and Sonnets* do not, of course, in any way
reflect the *Canzoniere's* sequential progression away from profane love, yet love's evil effects is undoubtedly one of Donne's
favorite motifs. The negative attitude toward love many of
his speakers directly express or unconsciously betray is a common
Petrarchan stance, even though Donne's lovers sometimes show
a perverse cynicism untypical of Petrarch generally. However,
four amorous abberrations can be identified in both poets—excessive grief, perversity, overindulgence, and self-deception—and
Donne's treatment of them suggests an awareness of the Pe-

trarchan precedent, if not a conscious attempt to imitate or, more accurately, ' parody,' Petrarch. To achieve a clearer perspective on and more accurate understanding of Donne's complex poetic method, unique effect, and persistent appeal, it is essential to re-evaluate Donne's *Songs* in terms of how they relate, directly and indirectly, to the Petrarchan love ethic with its stylized terminology and rhetoric.

Donne does not blanketly *deny* Petrarchism with its attendant conceits, paradoxes, and infantilisms. We can readily accept Lu Emily Pearson's claim in her classic study *Elizabethan Love Conventions* that Donne did not discard traditional conceits or satirize them as shallow or ridiculous, but rather " he sought to go beyond their conventional ideas, beyond the usual portrayal of love in order to find what is lurking in the shadows." In a sense Donne was in fact " independent of the revolt against Petrarchism " not only because he was interested in a more comprehensive vision of love than that reflected in Petrarch,[2] but also because he saw the value of the functional and positive use of Petrarchan elements.

Thus, Donne's relationship to the Petrarchan precedent is much more complex than commonly thought, for often he aggrandizes, complicates, or concretizes Petrarchan elements. Little has been done to uncover places where Donne employs Petrarchan analogues openly or where he uses their implications in order to determine to what extent and in what manner he concurs with or deviates from Petrarch. Donne's treatment of amorous abberrations offers a specific instance of how Petrarchan analogues function in his poetry and how they help determined its ultimate effect.

The most recurring of love's evil effects recognized by Donne and Petrarch is grief, which results ostensibly from disappointment, frustration, fear of inconstancy, or separation, among other sources. But ultimately the cause of the grief resides in the lover's obsessive worship of the lady. Donne's " Valediction: Of Weeping " dramatizes not only the grief at parting, but also the grief resulting from an idolatrous love. The treatment of this Petrarchan motif reflects Donne's variation of the language and thought of Petrarchan love.

A VALEDICTION: OF WEEPING

Let me powre forth
My teares before thy face, whil'st I stay here,
For thy face coines them, and thy stampe they beare,
And by this Mintage they are something worth,
    For thus they bee
    Pregnant of thee;
Fruits of much griefe they are, emblemes of more,
When a teare falls, that thou falls which it bore,
So thou and I are nothing then, when on a divers shore.

    On a round ball
A workeman that hath copies by, can lay
An Europe, Afrique, and an Asia,
And quickly make that, which was nothing, All,
    So doth each teare,
    Which thee doth weare,
A globe, yea world by that impression grow,
Till thy teares mixt with mine doe overflow
This world, by waters sent from thee, my heaven dissolved so.

    O more then Moone,
Draw not up seas to drowne me in thy spheare,
Weepe me not dead, in thine armes, but forbeare
To teach the sea, what it may doe too soone;
    Let not the winde
    Example finde,
To doe me more harme, then ti purposeth;
Since thou and I sigh one anothers breath,
Who e'r sighes most, is cruellest, and hasts the others death.

The first stanza focuses on the image of the weeping lover who must separate from his lady. The first two lines, with their stress on the words " powre forth," " teares," and " face " recall a similar first line in Petrarch's sonnet XVII, which treats the same motif, " Piovonmi amare lagrime dal viso." The hyperbole of Donne's opening lines is in keeping with the stance of grieving Petrarch, whose only pleasure in life is weeping, " Lagrimar sempre è 'l mio sommo diletto." Lines three through six of " The Valediction: Of Weeping " indicate that since his tears carry the lady's image, they assume more value. They carry her image because tears come from the eyes, which were thought to reflect the image of the beloved.[3] But Donne aggrandizes the

Petrarchan claim that the eyes reflect the beloved by making the same claim for the tears. The lover then makes the first of a series of comparisons to stress the lady's importance in his life. He says that her image on his tears gives them value, or " coines them " much in the same way as a King's face on a coin would add to its worth. But the statement following on its heels in line seven, that the tears are " fruits of much griefe... emblems of more," implies a darker side to this love-devotion. It suggests that the lover has suffered excessively in the past because of his total commitment to the lady, and he expects more suffering in the future, possibly in the form of betrayal during his absence. Undoubtedly, the line points to grief as an evil effect of his love for the lady, and it implies that the lover has lost faith in her constancy.[4] These fears are further substantiated in lines eight and nine, which anticipate that separation will have a negative effect on the lovers and their love.

The idea of the lady's importance, conveyed in stanza one by the coin-Mintage comparison, is continued in stanza two through the use of an extended analogy. She is portrayed first as a continent, " an Europe, Afrique, and an Asia; " then as a globe or world, and finally as a " heaven." But the Petrarchan claim that the lady is his world is set within an ironic context, for the lover sees this world soon to be drowned in a deluge of their mixed tears. By implication the lover will be destroyed along with his world, as he implies in the last words of the stanza, " my heaven dissolved so."

The speaker's foreboding of love's mutability and death becomes more explicit in the last stanza. He concretizes the suggestion in stanza two that the lady holds the power to destroy not only the lover, but also their world of love. Significantly, the lover calls his lady a " Moone," even " more than Moone," an appellation negatively suggesting vacillation, inconstancy, and coldness. It also implies its opposite, the sun, a frequent image in the *Canzoniere* used to refer positively to the lady, who warms the lover's world of love. As a moon, she is responsible for the sea tides which could drown the lover on the trip, so he begs her not to weep him dead. She should not teach the sea what it may well do soon enough. Nor should

she teach the wind how to do him harm, by sighing so much.
Her tears and her sighs could very well be the cause of his
death.⁶

   Much of what the lover says in this last stanza is drawn
from Petrarchan analogues. For example, in sonnet CCXVI, Petrarch describes how his own weeping will result in his death,
and how the lady refuses to save him from the certain death
to which his excessive grief has led him:

> Tutto 'l dí piango; et poi la notte, quando
> prendon riposo i miseri mortali,
> trovomi in pianto, et raddopiarsi i mali:
> cosí spendo 'l mio tempo lagrimando.
>
> In tristo humor vo li occhi consumando,
> e 'l cor in doglia; et son fra li animali
> l'ultimo, sí che li amorosi strali
> mi tengon ad ogni or di pace in bando.
>
> Lasso, che pur da l'un a l'altro sole,
> et da l'una ombra a l'altra, ò già 'l piú corso
> di questa morte, che si chiama vita.
>
> Piú l'altrui fallo che 'l mi' mal mi dole:
> ché Pietà viva, e 'l mio fido soccorso,
> védem' arder nel foco, et non m'aita.

Or again, sonnet XLI describes the effect of Laura's absence on
the whole universe, especially on the disturbance of the weather:

> Quando dal proprio sito si rimove
> l'arbor ch'amò già Phebo in corpo humano,
> sospira et suda a l'opera Vulcano,
> per rinfrescar l'aspre saette a Giove:
>
> il qual or tona, or nevicha et or piove,
> senza honorar piú Cesare che Giano;
> la terra piange, e 'l sol ci sta lontano,
> che la sua cara amica ved'altrove.
>
> Allor riprende ardir Saturno et Marte,
> crudeli stelle; et Orïone armato
> spezza a' tristi nocchier' governi et sarte;
>
> Eolo a Neptuno et a Giunon turbato
> fa sentire, et a noi, come si parte
> il bel viso dagli angeli aspectato.

In Donne's poems it is not so much the lady's absence that causes the weather disturbances—high tides and wind—but rather her weeping at the anticipated parting. In both poems, however, the main point is that the lady possesses the power to govern or control climatic conditions, and thereby the lover's world. Sonnet XXXVIII describes how Laura refuses to save him from death-by-weeping. Stressing the life-giving quality of her eyes, he tells her how by covering her eyes and refusing to look at him she condemns him to death. By such an act she implicitly condemns her lover to weep until he dies. The hand she uses to cover her eyes he compares to a large rock in the sea, which keeps him from staying on course as he travels homeward:

> Orso, e' non furon mai fiumi né stagni,
> né mare, ov'ogni rivo si disgombra,
> né di muro o di poggio o di ramo ombra,
> né nebbia che 'l ciel copra e 'l mondo bagni,
>
> né altro impedimento, onch'io mi lagni,
> qualunque piú l'umana vista ingombra,
> quanto d'un vel che due begli occhi adombra,
> et par che dica: Or ti consuma et piagni.
>
> Et quel lor inchinar ch'ogni mia gioia
> spegne o per humiltate o per argoglio,
> cagion sarà che 'nanzi tempo i' moia.
>
> Et quel lor inchinar ch'ogni mia gioia
> ch'è stata sempre accorta a farmi noia,
> et contra gli occhi miei s'è fatta scoglio.

" The Valediction: Of Weeping " expresses the passion of grief as one of the inevitable effects of an idolatrous earthly love in which the lover has placed too much faith and importance on a woman. Grief results not so much from the parting, as it does from the fact that the lady represents the lover's whole world. Parting only makes him realize the possibility of her future infidelity and of its destructive effect on their love. The poem is a study of the evil effects of grief on a Petrarchan lover, who allows himself to lose his free will and permits his fate to be determined by an idealized human being who has the power to destroy him and his world.

" Twicknam Garden " portrays " perversity " as an evil
effect of an unrequited love. The poem is a variation on the
Petrarchan sonnets which describe how Petrarch is not ennobled
by his love and in this respect both Petrarch and Donne deviate
from the ideal of courtly love. It bears a special resemblance
to those poems in which Petrarch describes how he undergoes
a metamorphosis as a result of his amorous obsession. Both
Donne and Petrarch use images of transformation or change
and comparisons with inanimate objects in order to portray love's
perverse and distorting effects. For example, in Petrarch's canzone XXIII, " Nel dolce tempo de la prima etade," which reflects Ovidian influence in recounting the various metamorphoses he underwent resulting from love, he describes how the
lady's scorn of his devotion has turned him into a stone—an
image conveying the coldness and frustration of unreciprocated
love:

> ed ella ne l'usata sua figura
> tosto tornando, fecemi, oimè lasso,
> d'un quasi vivo et sbigottito sasso.

(11. 78-80)

Later he is changed into a flint stone, which he believes is even
more lifeless than a normal stone:

> ch'ancor poi ripregando, i nervi et l'ossa
> mi volse in dura selce.

(11. 137-38)

The comparison is an apt one since the flint stone like the lover
possesses the capability to be ignited, but by remaining unused
this only increases his torment. The image also provides an
analogical definition of what is meant by *perversity* as an evil
effect of unrequited love. Although Petrarchan love possesses
a potential for good, often it is misdirected, wasted or turned
to an improper use with a destructive result. He then compares
his weeping over Laura's disdain to a fountain at the foot of
a beech tree. Again, in sonnet CXXXV, Petrarch compares himself to a strange fountain which boils only when the heat of the
sun departs (the *sun* here, of course, is Laura). During the day

the fountain waters become increasingly colder as the sun becomes hotter.

> Surge nel mezzo giorno
> una fontana, e tien nome dal sole,
> che per natura sòle
> bollir le notti, e 'n sul giorno esser fredda;
> e tanto si raffredda
> quanto 'l sol monta, et quanto è piú da presso.
>
> (11. 46-51)

Such an image is used to point to the perverse and abnormal
effects of unrequited love wrought on Petrarch's deprived physical and psychological condition.

The opening lines of Donne's " Twicknam Garden," with
their mention of sighs, tears, eyes, ears, balms, and cures for
love, immediately characterize the speaker as a Petrarchan lover,
but he is a " selfe traytor "—a lover who has betrayed himself
by loving one who does not love him in return. Instead of his
love turning bad to good and yielding virtuous effects, it has
done the reverse, turning good to bad and giving evil effects.
The lover is moved by the sight of a familiar place to speak
of his love and his lady. The situation here is similar to Petrarch's sonnet CCXLIII, " Fresco, ombroso, fiorito et verde colle," in which coming upon the place where he gave his heart
to Laura, he is moved by its sight to lament his miserable condition. He recounts how his rejected heart persists in abiding
with the cruel lady, who observes his plight with a smile on
her lips. He laments how his constant weeping has made him
as stupid and as insensible as a stone:

> Ella sel ride, et non è pari il gioco:
> tu paradiso, i'senza cor un sasso,
> o sacro, aventuroso et dolce loco.

The lovers in both sonnet CCXLIII and " Twicknam Garden "
are miserable over their unhappy loves. The ladies are portrayed
as unfeeling and unpitying, and thus, the lovers would rather
become some part of the landscape in order to escape the intensity of their sadness.

The speaker of " Twicknam Garden " further emphasizes
the perversity of this kind of love by calling it a " spider love,"
which as Gardner says refers to the spider turning all into
excrement and poison,[8] but may also suggest other perverse qualities associated with the spider which likewise bear comparison
to the speaker's love. The spider was classified in the ancient
category of *worms*, more comprehensive than the modern one.
Since like all worms, it was an animal which germinated without
sexual intercourse,[9] the speaker may be implying the perverse
nature of his unfulfilled sexuality. Petrarch also uses the spider
image in sonnet CLXXIII, which tells how love yields only
perversely bitter fruits from its ambiguous mixture of good
and bad seeds:

> quant'al mondo si tesse, opra d'aragna
> vede: onde seco et con Amor si lagna
> ch'à sí caldi gli spron', sí duro 'l freno.

Love here is pictured as something woven by the spider, that is,
shortlived and frail, but the image may also suggest the other
characteristics associated with the spider and probably commonly known from folklore. The speaker of " Twicknam Garden " heightens the perverse effects of his love suggested in
the Petrarchan context and probably derived from folklore by
twisting the Platonic claim that love transubstantiates bad into
good.

Lines 10-11 of " Twicknam Garden " emphasize the lover's
misery by alluding to the garden's springtime beauty, which
the lover wishes to replace with the cold dreariness of winter,
a setting more appropriate to his emotional state. The beauty
of the springtime garden serves as a dramatic contrast to the
misery of the lover's physical and psychological condition. As
in many of Petrarch's sonnets, the landscape is presented here
as a personified character who further externalizes the lover's
state. Petrarch often claims that Nature mocks him because it
is so beautiful and carefree while he is so deprived and miserable. The speaker of " Twicknam Garden " desires to become
" some senseless peece of this place," echoing Petrarch's similar
requests. His desire to become a weeping stone fountain recalls

Petrarch's strange fountain boiling only when the sun goes down. As a fountain he would act as a paragon for all lovers, who would go there with their " christall vyals " to taste of his tears. With these tears other lovers could test the sincerity of their mistress's tears, " For all are false, that tast not just like mine."

The last five lines of the poem are a generalized condemnation of women. The speaker repudiates the proverbial maxims that a woman's eyes will reflect what is in her heart, or that her tears reveal her true thoughts, as inapplicable in view of his own experience. He implies that theories of behavior cannot be used as accurate guides in a real situation because human nature is perverse and deceptive. The theoretical principles themselves are admirable and desirable, but human nature refuses to abide by them. Womankind is a " perverse sex," for it has twisted truth into an evil which works his death, and his play on the words " true " and " truth " in the last two lines emphasizes this perversity. The speaker suggests that the lady is unfaithful to him but constant to somebody else and his misery and rebuke of her derives from his knowledge of her perversity. Rebuke of the lady is not uncommon in Petrarch's *Canzoniere* and is consistent with his vacillation and conflicting emotions. Petrarch has a similar condemnation of womankind in sonnet CLXXXIII:

> Femina è cosa mobil per natura:
> ond'io so ben ch'un amoroso stato
> in cor di donna picciol tempo dura.

Donne's speaker is a disillusioned Petrarchan lover who desires a life founded upon the ideal rules, but who is forced to accept the evil and perverse distortion of ideals for personal advantage.

" Loves Diet " dramatizes the evil effect of overindulgence, elaborating the Petrarchan motif that love has grown to such an excessive degree that it threatens to devour the lover. The speaker in Donne's poem, unlike Petrarch, supposedly succeeds in overpowering Love and imprisoning him. He condemns Love to a limited ration of sighs and tears dictated by " that which love worst endures, *discretion*." By implication the lover and

his love invite comparison with Petrarch, who repeatedly
attempts a " diet " of discretion, but who fails time and again.
In the *Canzoniere* Petrarch is fully committed and devoted,
unable to control or restrain his passion. Since the lover of
Donne's poem says that he *has* put Love on a diet, we would
think that he is neither committed nor devoted. But indications
in the poem suggest that he is only fooling himself into thinking that he is different from the lover completely under Love's
control.

The characteristics of Petrarchan love which " Loves Diet "
attempts to repudiate are found in sonnets CXCVII, CCIX,
and canzone CCXIV. In sonnet CXCVII Petrarch describes how
totally he is entwined in love, how he is bound to Love by a
yoke around his neck, and how through overindulgence in his
obsessive commitment he has lost his freedom of action:

> L'aura celeste che 'n quel verde lauro
> spira, ov'Amor ferí nel fianco Apollo,
> et a me pose un dolce giogo al collo,
> tal che mia libertà tardi restauro,
>
> pò quello in me, che nel gran vecchio mauro
> Medusa quando in selce transformollo;
> né posso dal bel nodo omai dar crollo,
> là 've il sol perde, non pur l'ombra o l'auro:
>
> dico le chiome bionde, e 'l crespo laccio,
> che sí soavemente lega et stringe
> l'alma, che d'umiltate e non d'altr'armo.
>
> L'ombra sua sola fa 'l mio cor un ghiaccio,
> et di bianca paura il viso tinge;
> ma li occhi ànno vertú di farne un marmo.

Sonnet CCXI describes how against his will he is bound to this
unrequited love. He laments that he has allowed his sense,
and not his reason, to rule in the love relationship, reminding
us of Dante's line, " che la ragion sommettono al talento."
Explaining that the lady's graces " ai be' rami m'an giunto,"
he abandons all hope of ever regaining control and of finding
his way in this labyrinth of love:

> Voglia mi sprona, Amor mi guida et scorge,
> Piacer mi tira, Usanza mi trasporta,

> Speranza mi lusinga et riconforta
> et la man destra al cor già stanco porge;
>
> e 'l misero la prende, et non s'accorge
> di nostra cieca et disleale scorta:
> regnano i sensi, et la ragion è morta;
> de l'un vago desio l'altro risorge.
>
> Vertute, Honor, Bellezza, atto gentile,
> dolci parole ai be' rami m'àn giunto
> ove soavemente il cor s'invesca.
>
> Mille trecento ventisette, a punto
> su l'ora prima, il dí sesto d'aprile,
> nel laberinto intrai, né veggio ond'esca.

In canzone CCXIV, after all else fails, he finally begs God to restore the freedom lost from overindulgence, but the poem is only a request; it does not indicate any granting of the request:

> Ma Tu, Signor, ch'ài di pietate il pregio,
> porgimi la man dextra in questo bosco:
> vinca 'l Tuo sol le mie tenebre nove.
>
> Guarda 'l mio stato, a le vaghezze nove
> che 'nterrompendo di mia vita il corso
> m'àn fatto habitador d'ombroso bosco;
> rendimi, s'esser pò, libera et sciolta
> l'errante mia consorte; et fia Tuo 'l pregio,
> s'anchor Teco la trovo in miglior parte.
>
> Or ecco in parte le question mie nove:
> s'alcun pregio in me vive, o 'n tutto è corso,
> o l'alma sciolta, o ritenuta al bosco.

In each of the examples Love is personified as a creature independent of either lover or beloved, over which Petrarch has no control. Thus, Petrarch is unable to free himself of Love's entanglements, so his overindulgence has made love a source of pain rather than pleasure.

The lover in " Loves Diet " *seems* to have changed all that, for he sets out to disprove certain basic tenets of the Petrarchan position on love. First, he tries so show that Love is a creature within the control of man, who need not be its

victim, and secondly, he tries to prove that women are promiscuous and lascivious, not pure, ennobling, and faithful. He
attempts to do this by means of a little story, which we come
to realize is the history of his own love. The first stanza reveals
that he had once been an overindulgent Petrarchan lover, who
allowed his love to reach a state of " cumbersome unwieldi-
nesse / And burdenous corpulence," but unlike Petrarch he
realized the dangers of this kind of love, and he attempted to
" keepe it in proportion." The humor of the " overweight "
analogy veils the serious implications of the lines, which suggest that the speaker had at one time devoted himself totally
to a lady. In stanzas two, three, and four the speaker recounts
how he controlled Love's diet of sighs, tears, and love letters—
both those from himself and his lady. But in the case of the
lady, the diet really wasn't necessary, since her sighs were
" neither very sound, nor meant to me," her tears were a
" counterfeit " drink, since " eyes which rowle towards all,
weep not, but sweat," and her letters were only restatements
of what she had said to forty men on the list before him. What
the speaker is suggesting is that the diet might not have been
necessary if the lady had been as faithful and as devoted to
him as he was to her. His assertion of success in controlling
Love's weight is not quite convincing, for it offers only claims
and no proof, and it is tinged with resentment at the lady's
infidelity. He is not as free from Love's emotional involvement
as he would like us to believe, and his whole story of putting
Love on a diet of discretion is a clever way of veiling his
disillusionment with love and women. His story offers a distor-
ted picture of the tyrannical nature of love and of man's submission to it. We must recall that his competence in judging
Love or women is undermined not only by the failure to
present authoritative evidence, but also by his disillusioned
state of mind, which operates as the motivating force behind
his imposition of a diet on Love. Stanzas two, three, and four
reveal him to be a Petrarchan lover gone sour as a result of a
disappointing experience with a woman, to whom he had given
himself completely but overindulgently. Although the last stanza
vows a carefree, non-involved and negligent attitude toward love,

the vow is made much too easily. The poem is a humorous variation of the Petrarchan motif of overindulgence, when the object of devotion does not merit total commitment. The hyperbole and ridiculousness of the speaker's tale coupled with his flippant manner of presentation negates any reading of him as man who wants his story to be taken as a serious assertion of his love philosophy.[10] The meaning underlying the story is of real significance, the tale being merely used as a way of relieving the intensity of disappointment.

Related to the evil effects of grief, perversity and overindulgence is Petrarch's awareness that such a love is a deceptive folly. " The Baite " expresses such an awareness. The poem shows how Donne combines the ideal world of Petrarchan love with its romantic landscape of " golden sands," " christall brookes," " silken lines,," and " silver hookes," and the real world of actual experience with its " strangling snares " and " windowie nets." The speaker acknowledges the value and incommodities of both worlds. The poem turns on the image of the lady as a bait by which the lover is involuntarily drawn. Piscatorial imagery occurs so often in the *Canzoniere*, that it would be impossible to cite all the references, but a few will demonstrate the meaning and function of such imagery in Petrarch's sequence.

In sonnet CLXV Petrarch describes how Laura's physical beauty—her walk, look, words, and acts—are so much a lure for him, " ch'i' non curo altro ben né bramo altr'esca." The extent to which he is deceptively lured by her net of physical charms is further heightened by the seeming beauty of the landscape setting—the cool grass, the graceful flowers, and the invigorating sun. Beneath the external beauty of Laura and of the countryside abides the ominous fact that this love is fruitless, unreciprocated, and ultimately destructive. Sonnet CXCV describes how Petrarch is unable to drop the bit of hook and bait (" né però smorso i dolce inescati hami ") despite the fact that he is becoming older and " Di dì in dì vo cangiando il viso e 'l pelo." Petrarch asserts that he will love Laura until she requites him, or until death takes him. Sonnet CCXII laments that after twenty years of loving, love for his lady still ensnarls

him. The images of the bait (" esca ") and the hook (" amo ")
are clearly meant to symbolize the ambivalent and deceptive
mixture of sweetness and bitterness. In each of these poems
Petrarch's praise of the lady's beauty is ironically qualified by
the ominous suggestions of its deceptive and even murderous
quality and by the full recognition of the folly of his passion.[11]

Donne's " The Baite " follows these Petrarchan analogues
closely. It includes the hyperbolic praise of the lady—her eyes
which warm the river are brighter than the sun and all other
heavenly bodies—while at the same time suggesting that this
ideal world and ideal lady could bring death to the lover. The
last lines of the poem imply that he has allowed himself to be
lured because of his susceptibility to her physical charms. Both
Donne and Petrarch combine the praise of the lady's beauty
with recognition of the folly of their love. There is very little
new or original in Donne's treatment of love as a deceptive folly
in " The Baite."

" Loves Alchymie " is quite another matter, however. The
poem is a direct statement of the self-deceptive nature of love,
while offering an indirect commentary on love's other evil effects. " The Baite " merely restates a traditional view on love
with little originality, while " Loves Alchymie " uniquely varies
the same Petrarchan motif by means of concrete illustration and
intensification through analogy. It presents an evaluation of
" physical " and " spiritual " love in terms of how inadequate
they are in and of themselves.

The Petrarchan awareness of love's deception is concretely
projected in the first stanza by Donne's analogical use of alchemical concepts and language. Alchemy becomes a correspondence
for the illusory nature of profane love, and the indictment
against alchemy is an analogical substitution for an indictment
against love.[12] The speaker attempts to give his indictment of
love more authority and objectivity by relating it to another
area of human experience, but nonetheless, it is a condemnation
based on his own unfortunate personal experience.

The opening lines of " Loves Alchymie " reveal the speaker
to be a man who has apparently had extensive experience with
love, but who, nevertheless, feels that he is different from other

lovers, who " have deeper digg'd loves Myne then I." Despite
his substantial exposure to physical love, he has found it un-
satisfying as an end in itself. He bases his conclusions about
love on this experience, which would seem to give his statements
more authority and weight. But even though experience can
be a convincing corroboration of one's ideas, nevertheless, it
is also limiting, for someone else could have different experiences
and thus different conclusions. The only thing which his
experience really proves is that he has unfortunately had the
wrong type, and perhaps through some fault of his own. The
first of the two kinds of love which he condemns appears in
lines 2-4, indicating that love's " hidden mysterie " would never
be found if purely physical satisfaction were the end of the
quest. A lover who mistakes sex for love is as deluded as the
alchemist who mistakes a lesser substance for the elixir. The
fact that both the lover and the alchemist are self-deceivers is
summarized in the last couplet of the stanza. The lines contrast
the lover's " midsummer night's dream " of love with the cold
reality of deadening winter. The stanza as a whole reveals the
speaker's complete dissatisfaction with the physical aspects of
love as sole end.

The theme of self-deception is carried on in stanza two,
which presents a condemnation of that kind of love veiling its
physical desire by claims of spirituality. Whereas the focus of
attack in stanza one was profane love, in this stanza the speaker
attacks Platonic theory used to rationalize physical relationships.
Such a love is a " vaine Bubles shadow "—even less substantial
than either a shadow or bubble. It is the kind of love which
escapes from reality with the claim that " Tis not the bodies
marry, but the mindes." Its insubstantial quality is intensified
by combining two images which convey the idea of instability,
and the epithet is heightened by the derogatory adjective,
vaine, indicating the self-glorification such a lover desires. The
speaker's disillusionment with this kind of love's end result is
revealed in his statement that both he and his manservant
experience the same " happiness " with women. The speaker,
who considers himself more genteel and aristocratic, anticipated
a more elevated feeling from his love relationship. He ridicules

that " loving wretch "—an epithet for the Petrarchan lover—
who imagines that his marriage is one of the mind and not of
the body, and he frowns on the claims that women possess
angelic qualities. The lines are a stab at the Petrarchan assumption that the lover is a privileged and uniquely sensitive individual, and that his lady is above all earthly contamination. Here
we find the real cause of the speaker's cynicism. He has been
disillusioned by experience and he sees women's inadequacies
as the cause for love's failure. Women are not the spiritualizing
and inspirational force the theorists made them out to be. If
man seeks to ennoble himself through love of woman, he is
on as deceptive a quest as that of the alchemist.

But what the speaker is condemning is not so much alchemy [13] or love, whether physical or spiritual, in themselves,
but more their misuse by those who devote themselves to
either so indiscriminately and irresponsibly despite their dangers. Man channels all his creative efforts into the amorous
devotion of a lady—his " ease, thrift, honor and day "—only
to find that the object of the devotion was not worthy of the
commitment. The immoderate indulgence in physical love or the
unqualified loyalty to a spiritualized Petrarchan ideal are both
considered distortions of the true balance needed in a love
relationship. They are escapes from the claims of reality and
the needs of man.

" Loves Alchymie " expresses an amazing awareness of
love's self-deceptive power. It reveals how extreme positions or
attitudes may prevail in a love relationship in the guise of
something else. Lovers, both " physical " and " spiritual," often
fool themselves into thinking that their physical love is more
spiritual or that their spiritual love is more physical than in
reality. Complete commitment to and overindulgence in either
kind of love is inadequate and even self-destructive, for either
could eventually lead to the perversity of alienating man from
his essential humanity. The speaker's attack is equally divided
between lustful and idealized love, and his purpose is to reveal
the self-deceiving quality of both. Thus, the poem is an indirect
call for balance and moderation in love in order to avoid its
abberrations.

" Farewell to Love " demonstrates what happens to a
lover who has been consumed by perversity, overindulgence,
and self-deception. Although the poem's title claims it is a
Petrarchan renunciation of love, the subtle implications of its
content ironically undercut its form. Petrarch repeatedly, but
unsuccessfully, vows to free himself of love (see sonnets CXCVII,
CCIX, canzone CCXIV). In canzone CXLII he pleads:

> mostranmi altro sentier di gire al cielo
> et di far frutto, non pur fior' et frondi.
> altr'amor, altre frondi et altro lume,
> altro salir al ciel per altri poggi
> cerco, ché n'è ben tempo, et altri rami.

In sonnet LXII he asks God, " piacciati omai col tuo lume
ch'io torni / ad altra vita et a più belle imprese." Sonnets
LXXVI and LXXXI express the same awareness of love's flat-
teries and self-deception, and Petrarch's desire to rid himself
of that " fascio antico."

Donne allows his speaker to use the form of the Petrarchan
renunciation of profane love in favor of a higher love as an
ironic context within which to view his statements. In the
first stanza the lover says that he has found the promises of
pleasure and joy in profane love to be more illusions, and that
his experience with love has proven the theories to be lies. But
we soon discover that the speaker is not what he says he is.
He has attempted to portray himself as a disillusioned Petrarchan
lover who has wisely found profane love to fall short of any
of his ideals. Specifically, he voices his disillusionment with
purely sexual love, but we soon begin to question the sincerity
of his " farewell to love." His use of religious imagery in the
first stanza recalls implications of his idolatrous devotion to
earthly love. The force of his condemnation of physical love
is heightened by his " atheists " analogy, which suggests that
his reverencing of love is to be viewed in a godless or pagan
context. His language in stanza one betrays his secret preoccupa-
tion with sex. His choice of such words as " crave," " coveted,"
" desires," " sise " [14] suggests physical love despite the apparent
attempt to condemn love by means of the " atheists " analogy.

In stanza two he grieves that once physical desire is sated, " Being had, enjoying it decayes... it leaves behinde / A kinde of sorrowing dulnesse to the mind." We would expect now, if the poem were true to form, the Petrarchan vow to renounce this kind of love. Instead the speaker expresses, perhaps unwittingly, his nostalgic desire to be like cocks and lions which were reputed to suffer no " sorrowing dulnesse to the mind " following intercourse. His complaints about its dulling effects and about its brevity suggest his veiled desire to better the sex act in order to improve and lengthen his pleasure. The apparent vow to reform, " I'll no more dote and runne / To pursue things which had, indammage mee," is undercut by a series of implications inherent in his statements. His claims to desire sex because it fulfills his need for offspring is in reality a veiling of his desire for more sex. In the last stanza he says that if all else fails to help renounce love, then he will use the sex act as a deterrent to further physical desire, but his statement undercuts the sincerity of his vow to reform. The speaker is not, like Petrarch, a convert to a higher form of love. He is a man caught in a circle of lust from which there is no escape, and he ends up in the poem exactly where he started—a victim of his own hedonism. He merely gives lipservice to Petrarch's vow to reform, but the forcefulness of his vow is debilitated by his acknowledgment of possible failure, to which he seemingly adjusts easily. The speaker is a condemned man who vows, not to devote himself to a higher love, but to persist and intensify in his present activity. By implication, then, he is not saying " farewell to love " at all, for the substance of his statements undermines the poem's form. Although we expect a renunciation of love, instead we get a veiled call for continuance in " love," and we unconsciously find ourselves comparing his statements with those of Petrarch.

A comparison of amorous abberrations in Petrarch and Donne reveals that often the ideals and the effects of Petrarchan love prevail in Donne's *Songs* relatively unchanged. The uniqueness of Donne's treatment of these stock motifs resides in his dramatic juxtaposition of Petrarchan ideals to the real world, in his frequent use of an ironic persona, who seemingly accepts but may undercut Petrarchan values, and in his making of new associations or combinations between the world of ideal love and the world of reality which do not appear in Petrarch. The Petrarchan code, behavior, and language operate in Donne as the basis for creative adaptation rather than as objects of pure satiric rejection.

IV. DREAMS, MEMORIES, AND FANTASIES

Petrarch's immensely graphic imagination allows him to survive despite constant rejection and despite the hopelessness of his continued devotion. Although his actual experience with the lady lacks any substantial fulfillment, his imagination supplies what reality and experience have denied. Through his imagination he forgets the pain of separation or of insensitive treatment. If he is absent from his lady, he imagines her near and it consoles his grief (CXXX). If she is near, he imagines that she reciprocates his love (CXXVI). If she has been cruel, he imagines a delicate revenge (CXXI). If she has been conciliatory, he savors the sweetness of future conciliations. His imagination acts as the link between things as they are and things as he would like them to be.

The imagination, manifesting itself as dream, recollection, or fantasy, offers the despairing Petrarch a comforting escape from the pain of reality. His need for the enjoyment of fantastical imaginings reflects his desire to forget himself and his sorrow. Frederick Goldin, in tracing this motif in the Provençal lyricists, says that " the poet turns to the consolation of the dream and the fantasy—an imaginary *mise-en-scène*... less present than the real but more present than the merely possible," by which " the fantasy replaces the thought of action." [1] Although Petrarch enjoys contemplating his imaginings, he is, nevertheless, acutely aware of the distinct difference between reality and imagination. It is his dissatisfaction with reality which motivates his creation of an imaginary world in which he represents some aspects as real and others (such as his image of the lady and his dream of winning her), as illusory. Ultimately, Petrarch's fantasizing on his idealized devotion reflects his awareness that his love, though worthy, conflicts with the lessons of experience.

Petrarch's vivid imagination allows him to recall the place, time, and circumstances when first he saw Laura, or when she first granted him her salute (CIX). It allows him to see Laura as a child, not of the earth, but of heaven. He forgets the detachment and disciplined restraint of her real self, which has caused him so much pain, and he indulges instead in a transcendental vision of her divine self (CXXVI, 11. 55-56). Even when conversing with other women, he finds himself drifting off into a fantastic reverie of Laura's pleasing image (CXLIII). In his imaginary world Laura is an " angel " and a " miracle." Often the imagination works on the memory to make him recall some significant incident in the love history as though it were actually present to him, as in sonnet CLVII, when he remembers the time he first saw Laura cry. At other times, the imagination offers dreary omens of future sadness and tragedy, as in sonnet CCXLIX, in which his recollection of a painful past separation provokes a vision of a future time when separation actually means a real death. In all cases, the imagination is the instrument by which Laura's image is constantly kept before him, as he affirms in CLVIII, which describes how she has totally possessed his senses and thoughts and how no matter where he turns his eyes he envisions her. The motif of the imagination points out Petrarch's obsessive concern for the lady, who powerfully controls his total being.

Donne's *Songs* reveal a Petrarchan concern for the power and the effects of the lover's imagination.[2] Three of his poems deal entirely with the motif, " The Dreame," " The Apparition," and " Image and Dream," while several deal with it indirectly, as in " The Good-morrow," " The Dampe," " The Relique," and " The Funerall," among others. An analysis of how Donne adapts this Petrarchan motif reveals to what extent he valued the real and the ideal worlds, and what relationships he saw between them. Petrarch's awareness of the discrepancy between the imagined and the actual becomes even more striking in Donne, who, while frequently evoking a fantasy world, paints the details of the real world more dramatically than Petrarch. Like Petrarch, Donne's speakers sometimes use the imagination as an escape from reality to where they can fulfill their most

secret or most outrageous desires. The imagination as dream,
apparition, or fantasy becomes a vivid projection of a lover's
innermost desires and anxieties.

In these poems Donne also deals with the relationship of
semantics, or language, to reality and to the imaginative powers
of the mind. The poems provide a commentary on the notion
that one can say or imagine what he pleases, but reality remains
reality. Or does it? Do the excursions into fantasy have any
appreciable effect on the " real " world? Can language, a product
of thought and imagination, influence reality? These poems trace
a movement referred to by one Donne critic as the " old beginning redefined by experience," but the redefinition of the " old
beginning " results not from direct experience, but from the
fantastical workings of the imagination. The conclusion of this
imaginative experience " yields the new knowledge that the place
is preciously, if painfully, different from where one started.[3]
Thus, the journey from reality into fantasy and back again as
described by language can result in a change in the initial
starting point by modifying one's perception of it, or by actually
changing it in some way. It is in this area of yielding " new
knowledge " about reality and fantasy that Donne makes one
of his significant contributions to the Petrarchist tradition.
Although Petrarch is aware of the differences between the real
and the imaginary, he is helpless to escape the mendacity of
the mirror of the imagination. He remains a prisoner of barren
illusions and a passive observer of its fleeting scenes. His awareness is never transformed into action, and the destinations of
his fantastical journies are no different from the departures. But
in Donne, imagination becomes a lived " experience," not merely
an escape. In the end it liberates the lover from the inertia of
pure observation, extreme self-consciousness, and painful passivity. In these poems Donne reevaluates the pertinence of
Petrarchan modes of expression to reality and to man's imaginative transformation of reality. Unlike Petrarch's, Donne's
flights into fantasy do not perpetuate the irreconcilable chasm
between real and imagined; instead, he effects an acceptable
adjustment of real and ideal, of actual and imagined. He accomplishes this adjustment by showing a real encounter with

the lady in terms of and in the light of idealized Petrarchan language and sentiment.

" The Apparition " applies the language and sentiment of Petrarchan love to an imagined experience which the lover hopes will in some way change reality. It demonstrates that Donne's application of Petrarchan language to a realistic sexual encounter does not necessarily mean that he is parodying or denouncing the language and sentiment of idealized love.

> When by thy scorne, O murdresse, I am dead,
> And that thou thinkst the free
> From all solicitation from mee,
> Then shall my ghost come to thy bed,
> And thee, fain'd vestall, in worse armes shall see;
> Then thy sicke taper will begin to winke,
> And he, whose thou art then, being try'd before,
> Will, if thou stirre, or pinch to wake him, thinke
>   Thou call'st for more,
> And in false sleepe will from thee shrinke,
> And then poore Aspen wretch, neglected thou
> Bath'd in a cold quicksilver sweat wilt lye
>   A veryer ghost then I;
> What I will say, I will not tell thee now,
> Lest that preserve thee; 'and since my love is spent,
> I'had rather thou shouldst painfully repent,
> Then by my threatnings rest still innocent.

The well-known shocking effect of the poem results from its application of Petrarchan conceits, which Petrarch uses to heighten his often desperate emotional state, to a situation in which Donne's speaker imagines the conceits to be acted out to their conclusions. The speaker takes the thought behind the conceits of death through unrequited love (" When by thy scorne, O murdresse I am dead "), the supernatural punishment of a cruel lady (" Then shall my ghost come to thy bed "), and the rejected lover's desire for revenge (" What I will say, I will not tell thee now, / Lest that preserve thee ") and carries it beyond Petrarch's figurative or symbolic portrayal. The effect is made highly dramatic by the extension into a real situation of the conceits appearing within the context of an imagined scene, in which the frustrated, unrequited lover contemplates

a revenge on his cruel lady. Donne uses the Petrarchan motif
of the lover's vivid imagination to deal with a real situation.
The speaker seeks this imagined revenge because in reality the
lady has denied him what she has apparently granted some
other. In his imagination he accomplishes what he seems unable
to do in real life, doing so with the secret hope that the imagined
threat will somehow change his lady.

Petrarch treats the revenge theme in madrigal CXXI, but
there is a difference in the way revenge is achieved and who
achieves it. The poem is addressed to the God of Love, whom
the speaker reminds of his lady's cruelty. He builds his case
against the lady by warning Love,

> tuo regno sprezza, et del mio mal non cura,
> et tra duo ta' nemici è sí secura.

> Tu se' armato, et ella in treccie e 'n gonna
> si siede, et scalza, in mezzo i fiori et l'erba,
> ver' me spietata, e 'ncontra te superba.

He also reminds Love that he is helpless to do anything about
his unfortunate state, since " I' son pregion." He begs Love,
who is armed with bow and arrow, to " fa' di te et di me,
signor, vendetta." But the kind of revenge he is seeking is
that the lady, wounded by Love's arrow, will reciprocate his
love. In sonnet CCLVI Petrarch desires revenge against his
lady, who cruelly destroys him by her look and her speech.

> Far potess'io vendetta di colei
> che guardando et parlando mi distrugge,
> et per piú doglia poi s'asconde et fugge,
> celando li occhi a me sí dolci et rei.

> Cosí li afflicti et stanchi spirti mei
> a poco a poco consumando sugge,
> e 'n sul cor quasi fiero leon rugge
> la notte allor quand'io posar devrei.

> L'alma, cui Morte del suo albergo caccia,
> da me si parte, et di tal nodo sciolta,
> vassene pur a lei che la minaccia.

> Meravigliomi ben s'alcuna volta,
> mentre le parla et piange et poi l'abbraccia,
> non rompe il sonno suo, s'ella l'ascolta.

He is torn by the sweetness and cruelty of her eyes, a detail which suggests her ambiguous nature. The ambiguity is further heightened when he tells how at night she comes to haunt his heart as a growling lion would taunt his prey.[4]

Donne combines this theme of the lover's revenge with that of the lover's imagination, and his treatment of both seems to yield a completely new kind of poem in " The Apparition." Unlike Petrarch, Donne's speaker imagines working the revenge directly himself. He seems to have nothing in common with Petrarch, who is a helpless captive. Donne's speaker rejects mere lamentation of his miserable state, and vows to do something about it himself. Yet when we look more closely at the conclusion of " The Apparition " and its motivating circumstance, we find that it is not so very different from Petrarch's madrigal or sonnet after all. The " revenge " Petrarch seeks is reciprocated love because he dearly loves the lady. With Donne's speaker we perceive a man whose heartless revenge would seem to say that he no longer loves the lady, but we suddenly recall that the speaker is imagining a time when he will be dead because of her cruelty. As Gardner notes, " for if he no longer loves her why should her cruelty kill him? "[5] Thus Donne's lover desires the same kind of " revenge " as Petrarch—reciprocated love. There is no repudiation of Petrarchan commitments, even though the language of Petrarchan love is applied in a new and dramatic way. He unconsciously hopes that his talking about an imagined revenge will in some way make his lady love him. He secretly desires that the imaginative experience will have some effect on reality.

In " The Apparition the speaker uses the imagination as a way of dealing constructively with reality, rather than escaping it. The striking contrasts implicit throughout the poem between real and ideal emphasize that he has his eyes fixed on changing reality, even though he seems to be simply indulging in sadistic fantasy. We find ourselves comparing the realistic and sensual protagonists of this situation with the idealized love and protagonists in Petrarch's sequence. Donne's intimate bedroom setting and " fain'd vestall " are a far cry from Petrarch's arcadian landscape and miraculous Laura. Donne's poem also

suggests that the lady's refusal has effected diabolical transformations on the lover, who has become a revenging ghost uttering
magical curses. Contrast this with Petrarch's realization near the
end of his sonnet sequence that his lady's scorn had benevolent
spiritual effects on him of which he was at the time unaware.[6]
These implied contrasts suggest that Donne's speaker has faced
reality squarely, not escaped from it. Although he is dissatisfied
with reality, this confrontation does not discourage him from
trying to change it, and the imagination is the instrument by
which he attempts to make the change. The speaker of " The
Apparition " indulges in no falsification of the motives and
needs of love through the imaginative experience. Yet he is a
Petrarchan lover who loves his lady, despite her faults, her
scorn and infidelity, but who actively tries to make her love
him. But we wonder if she is worth all his effort.

" The Dreame " is a variation of the Petrarchan sonnets
on the lover's nocturnal imaginings. Sonnet CCXXIII describes
how Petrarch, unrequited and unable to sleep, spends his nights
in tearful lamentation relieved only by the fantastical vagaries of
his mind. Sonnet CLXIV complains of how all other earthly
creatures use the night for rest, while he spends in " sol di lei
pensando." " The Dreame " resembles Petrarch's sonnet CCLIV,
which describes how the lady comes to haunt his thoughts at
night, how she ignites his amorous desires, only to quench them,
not with sweet fulfillment, but with bitter rejection.

Donne's poem builds on the themes of these Petrarchan
analogues. The speaker describes how the overwhelming power
of his lady's eyes woke him from his erotic dream of her, but
he is not sorry since he hopes that with her presence, he can
continue the dream in reality. The subject of this lover's dream
is much less pure in its intent toward the lady than any of
Petrarch's dreams, but we cannot ignore the sexual overtones
of Petrarch's nocturnal fantasies. Difficulties in interpretation
arise when Donne's use of Petrarchan conceits is not made
clear in the light of Petrarchan analogues. For example, the
speaker's description of his lady in stanzas one and two confirms
his desire to combine the real and the ideal. He supplements
the Petrarchan conceits used to describe her with more realistic

references. He deifies her by comparing her with " truth " [7] or
by calling her an angel, but he qualifies these idealized Petrarchan
claims by saying that the " real " lady possesses many more
superior qualities than any angel:

> I doe confesse, it could not chuse but bee
> Prophane, to think thee anything but thee.

Later in lines 27-30 the speaker of " The Dreame " offers an
explanation of the lady's function in his dream, which conforms
to the Petrarchan idea that the lady inflames the imagination
with passion. In the *Canzoniere* this passion remains bridled or
unfulfilled because of Petrarch's passive nature, but nevertheless,
the passion is there. Compare Donne's lines:

> Thou cam'st to kindle, goest to come; Then I
> Will dreame that hope againe, but else would die.

with Petrarch's

> Cosí li afflicti et stanchi spirti mei
> a poco a poco consumando sugge.
>
> (CCLVI)

Both examples associate the unrequited flames of passion with
the lover's death. Donne's poem supplies the realism of an
actual encounter with the lady, something which Petrarch's
sonnet lacks, but the basic idea is the same. Both lovers desire
fulfillment, yet Donne's poem takes this idea a step further into
the real world. " The Dreame " shows how he extends and
completes the Petrarchan concept of love by adding the body
to the mind, by supplementing the dream, a product of the
lover's imagination, with reality. Donne does not reject idealizing passion simply because he applies its motifs or conceits to
sexual encounters. Rather, his treatment of the motif of the
lover's imagination shows how he goes beyond the idealizing
passion by carrying out the thought behind its conceits. The
relationship between imagination and reality in Donne's poem
is different from that in Petrarch. Petrarch's dream remains
within the realm of pure fantasy, while in Donne it becomes

actualized in real life. Petrarch's dreams are a substitute for
reality; Donne's dreams begin a movement which he hopes
reality will complete. The speaker of Donne's poem uses the
dream as a way of changing reality by convincing the lady to
return his love.

"Image and Dream" provides another example of how
Donne supplements the imagination with reality. The word
"image" is used as a synonym for "reality," which is opposed
to "dream." The fantasy offers the fulfillment which reality
has denied, yet his apparent rejection of the idealized but unrequited love situation in favor of an imagined but sexually fulfilled love is only temporary. At the end of the poem the speaker
returns to the idealized notion, reassuming the Petrarchan pose
of the meditative lover, but not without some change.

The first stanza defines the love situation and protagonists
as essentially Petrarchan by the speaker's allusion to his unwanted heart, on which he carries his lady's "faire impression."
However, the lover is dissatisfied with this state of affairs.
Asserting Petrarch's frequent claim that the dream is more
satisfying than reality, he decides to escape into a fantasy world
where his love is sexually fulfilled. An implied paradox throughout the poem is that the lover's contemplation of his lady's
image on his heart is as much a dream as his "Fantasie"
dream is. Stanza two presents the lover's imaginings, freed from
the pains of the real relationship:

> So, if I dreame I have you, I have you,
>   For, all our joyes are but fantasticall.
> And so I scape the paine, for paine is true.

For a time he succumbs to the Petrarchan weakness of allowing
fantasy to supplant fruitless reality, to become his "Queene
and Soule, and all." Although his Fantasie has become a kind
of rival mistress who unlike the real mistress returns his love,
the speaker is never really satisfied with this solution. He realizes
he cannot permanently escape reality through the fantasy. Yet
paradoxically it is his very indulgence in fantasy which allows
him to arrive at this awareness. He says in stanza three that
the imagined experience has given him new knowledge about

his real love affair and has clarified his thinking about the nature of love. He rejects a total escapist commitment to the imagination, while he acknowledges that it has influenced reality in several positive ways. Specifically, it has helped him to write better love sonnets, but more importantly it has given him a new insight into his original situation:

> Fill'd with her love, may I be rather grown
> Mad with much heart, then ideott with none.

Realizing that the fantasy is a baser faculty than reason, he prefers the " madness " of rational contemplation of her image to the " ideocy " of intangible fantasizing. The speaker has made a journey from the painful reality of his unwanted heart into the illusory world of sexual fulfillment, and back again, but his perception of the starting point has been altered by the intervening imaginative experience, which has forced him to reevaluate the relationship between fantasy and reality. He has weighed the relative merits of an imagined world of love, in which all his sensual desires are fulfilled, and the real world of love, in which his love is painful and frustrating, but idealized, and he has decided on the latter. Line 21 indicates a definite turn in the poem, emphasizing that the speaker has only toyed with the possibility of abandoning an idealized love. He has seen value in both and has not rejected either. In this poem Donne displays the gift of seeing both sides of the coin. He shows his concern with how well the Petrarchan idealized language and sentiment can be adapted to man's human condition and to his normal human needs. Neither the rational nor the sensual, neither " image " nor " dream " is sufficient in itself for a balanced vision of man in love.

V. SUNS AND LOVERS

Donne's " The Sunne Rising " presents a dramatic reconciliation of the sterile world of Petrarchan adoration with the
fruitful world of reciprocated love. Donne here and in a few
other poems (" The Good-morrow " and " Loves Growth ")
struggles to define the nature of that kind of love which would
be " ideal " for the person living an active, fulfilling existence.
It is a love which gratifies the needs of spirit and body, in
accord with the realities of life while at the same time seeking
to transcend time and earthly limitations. In short, Donne
attempts to adjust the remote and passive Petrarchan vision of
love to the necessities of actual existence.

However, the poem's unique effect results from Donne's
skillful manipulation and synthesis of conventional Petrarchan
motifs within a traditional medieval form. The situation it
dramatizes, the solution it offers, and the language by which
both are projected can be understood more clearly once viewed
within the context of Petrarchan motifs, idiom, and behavior
which the poem reshapes. Except for the colloquial and play-
fully abusive rhetoric directed at the sun especially in the early
lines (" Busie old foole, unruly Sunne "), the subject of the poem
is neither original nor revolutionary. What *is* innovative is the
unusual way Donne combines Petrarchan ingredients, extending
and redefining them to produce a poem offering an insight into
his mature vision of love as a feasible reconciliation of time
with eternity.

Often Donne has been judged as an iconoclastic innovator
rejecting conventional modes, especially Petrarchan ones, when
in fact he often summarizes the love traditions he knew so well.
This becomes evident when we compare Donne's adaptation of
the *alba* form in " The Sunne Rising," and specifically his use
of the sun image, with Petrarch's treatment of the same form

and image. Such a comparison demonstrates how Donne assimilated and transmogrified the Petrarchan mode, indicating
that his debt to Petrarch may be greater than has been previously
acknowledged in traditional criticism. It offers some insight into
the precise relationship between the imitative and unique elements in Donne's poetry, while suggesting alternate readings of
his *Songs* as a whole by the comparison with the broader
Petrarchan context.

As has been often noted, "The Sunne Rising" creatively
reshapes the traditional *alba* in which the lover awakes next
to his beloved after a night of love lamenting that they must
part. What has been unnoticed is the similarity of this poem
to Petrarch's treatment of the same subject. Despite the seemingly unrequited nature of Petrarch's love as described in the
Canzoniere, he too treats the motif in sonnet CCXIX which
tells how he is awakened in the morning by singing birds and
a brilliant sun:

> Il cantar novo e 'l pianger delli augelli
> in sul dí fanno retentir le valli,
> e 'l mormorar de' liquidi cristalli
> giú per lucidi, freschi rivi et snelli.
>
> Quella ch'a neve il volto, oro i capelli,
> nel cui amor non fur mai inganni né falli,
> destami al suon de li amorosi balli,
> pettinando al suo vecchio i bianchi velli.

The sonnet is undoubtedly an *alba* characterized by the
veiled and elegant incorporation of sexual overtones in the
language used to describe setting and protagonists.[1] Petrarch
achieves ambivalence by allegorizing his situation with Laura
through the myth of Aurora (or Eos, as she is sometimes called)
and Tithonus. The lines cited are a reworking of classical
descriptions in Homer, Apollodorus, Hesiod and others of how
the goddess Dawn arose from her bed where she lay beside
Tithonus to bring light into the world.[2] Petrarch metaphorically
compares the details and the significance of this myth to his
own amorous predicament. The sonnet appears late in the
sequence of those written during the life of Madonna Laura,

in fact, after some twenty years of Petrarch's unmitigating devotion. More study needs to be done on the structural and thematic
function of classical imagery in Petrarch's *Canzoniere*, but from
a consideration of this poem alone we can conclude that the
myth operates within this sonnet as more than just beautifying
and uplifting but essentially meaningless decoration. As in the
myth, Petrarch's lines suggest the possibility of a bedroom scene
where the lovers awaken together after a night of love. Laura,
like her mythological counterpart, is eternally fresh and beautiful
(" Quella ch'a neve il volto, oro i capelli "); however, Petrarch,
also like his mythological counterpart, laments that he is growing older and greyer with each day (" pettinando al suo vecchio
i bianchi velli "). Through the elegant device of the classical
myth, Petrarch disguises his anxieties about age, sexual impair-
ment, and poetic decline. The image of the greying hair suggests both the lover's fear of encroaching sexual impotence and
the poet's fear of progressive artistic failure. It alludes to the
recurring theme in the *Canzoniere* of how the poet can conquer
the effects of time, and it functions to reaffirm Petrarch's alliance
between his love for Laura and his desire for poetic fame. Like
Tithonus, who had been granted immortality but not perpetual
youth,[3] Petrarch may have immortality through his art, but he
inescapably remains a mortal, decaying poet-lover struggling to
conquer time through poetic creativity.

Here Petrarch conspicuously does not lament his more
commonly accepted posture, that of the frustrated, complaining
adulator; instead the line " nel cui amor non fur mai inganni
né falli " implies the reciprocated nature of the love. The relationship described here is neither marked by deceptive game-
playing nor is it an ephemeral, chance coitus. The sexual overtones are further heightened by the implicit comparison of
the lovers' motions of love to the dancing of the birds in the
line, " destami al suon de li amorosi balli." The birds represent
the outside world functioning as the first dawn harbingers. The
effect created by the description of the arcadian landscape outside
the lovers' little world—the chirping birds, the murmuring
crystalline waters, the rising sun—is to sanction the ritualistic

events and protagonists inside the bedroom as in accord with the recurrent rhythms of nature.

In his word portrait of the glorious arrival of dawn (" l'aurora " is a play on Laura's name), Petrarch calls his lady another " sun," more potent in her attempts to revitalize his blinding desire despite his aging than the real sun is in revitalizing the world:

> Cosí mi sveglio a salutar l'aurora,
> E 'l sol ch'è seco, et piú l'altro ond'io fui
> ne' primi anni abagliato e son ancora.

The idea of the lady as a " sun " more powerful and even successful than Nature's sun is common in Petrarch, appearing, for example, in sonnet IX in which he compares the effect of Laura's eyes on him to that of the sun's beams on the earth. Just as the sun provides warmth and life, so Laura's eyes " Cria d'amor penseri, atti." However, Nature's sun despite its power possesses limitations, for it is a representative of the ephemeral real world, and as such can merely extinguish the light of the fading stars in the cosmos. On the other hand, Laura, as a symbolic sun in the immutable world of love, can outshine the brilliancy of the sun itself:

> I'gli ò veduti alcun giorno ambedui
> Levarsi inseme, e 'n un punto e 'n un' hora
> Quel far le stelle, et questo sparir lui.
>
> -CCXIX

This remarkable poem demonstrates how Petrarch's love can on occasion, despite the ambivalence of his veiled language, broach the possibility of a mutual, sexually fulfilled relationship. When it does, the fulfillment of an actual encounter with the lady functions to heighten the quality of the vision of perfect fulfillment which the lover harbored for so long in his imagination. The sonnet shows how Petrarch uses the *alba* form to present an extravagant praise of his lady, enhancing her at the expense of the real world outside which merely buttresses his ideal vision of love. The praise indicates that the real world of

nature and human activity has more meaning because of the
lady, an incarnation of the ideal. But the sonnet implicitly
shows how Petrarch accepts the inevitable claims and limitations
of this world on the world of love, for he envisions himself as
an aged Tithonus.

By the use of direct, unequivocal language Donne renders
more overt the sexual ambiguities of the Petrarchan context.
As in Petrarch's sonnet, Donne's opening lines establish the
bedroom setting with its amorous protagonists. But unlike
Petrarch, he is more concerned with showing how this intimate
world of love differs from the world beyond the curtained
windows. In Petrarch's poem the world outside is basically one
of rural beauty nurturing and sustaining his ideal love, while
in Donne's poem it is composed of mundane pedants and tardy
school boys detracting from his ideal.[4] However, both stress
the point, made more explicit in Donne, that the microcosm
of reciprocated love attempts to exist according to its own self-
sufficient rules.

In stanza two Donne follows the Petrarchan pattern of
contrasting his lady to the sun, who represents the world of
change, concluding that her potent eye-beams could blind even
the sun's. (Petrarch uses the Italian equivalent, *abagliato*.)
Donne extends Petrarch's praise of Laura's snow-white complex-
ion and golden hair into a hyperbolic catalogue of qualities his
lady embodies, all drawn from the macrocosm and epitomized
in her. But Donne's image of the lady is as idealized as Petrarch's
ever was in the *Canzoniere*:

> If her eyes have not blinded thine,
> Looke, and to morrow late, tell mee
> Whether both the' India's of spice and Myne
> Be where thou liftst them, or lie here with mee.
> Aske for those Kings whom thou saw'st yesterday,
> And thou shall heare, all here in one bed lay.

The exaggeration functions to disparage both the world beyond
their room and the role of the sun in that world. Donne's
lover frankly complains that dawn has interrupted the lovers'

amorous activity, while Petrarch more discreetly wakes to greet
the dawn. Donne could make distinctions between the real
dawn and his lady which in Petrarch are not permitted, for
he preserves the delicate courtly atmosphere of secrecy and
discretion. Petrarch cloaks his physical proximity to the lady
and marks her behavior toward him by " metaphorizing " her
as a sun and by identifying her with the mythic Aurora.

But in sonnet CCLV Petrarch also recognizes the importance of night to lovers:

> La sera desïare, odiar l'aurora
> soglion questi tranquilli et lieti amanti.

Unlike Donne, Petrarch is not always a tranquil, happy lover;
so often for him, " ... doppia la sera et doglia et pianti," since
with night both his " suns " disappear. His love is idealized and
more frequently unreciprocated, thus the night is usually a time
of forced separation from his married lady. Donne's treatment
of the *alba* in " The Sunne Rising " in this respect is even more
conventional than Petrarch's, since Donne affirms a convention
of the form which Petrarch's usually unrequited love will not
permit. It is not uncommon for Petrarch to lament the arrival
of night, as in sonnet CCXXIII which describes how he spends
" un'angosciosa et dura notte " in the company only of the
sky, stars, and moon, when he would rather be in the arms of
his beloved. Few have noticed that Petrarch's repeated complaining about the difficulties of the night suggests that he longs
for sexual fulfillment which night usually promises and brings
to mutual lovers.

" The Sunne Rising " also presents a fictional confrontation
between the lover and the sun, but such mythical encounters
are not uncommon in Petrarch's sequence. For example, in
sonnet CXV Petrarch imagines himself as a rival of the sun,
jealously competing for the lady's affections. She must decide
between the " human " lover and " quel signor... / che fra
gli uomini regna et fra li dei." Both " The Sunne Rising " and
sonnet CXV are challenges to the sun, but Petrarch refers to
the sun as " l'amico più bello," who beguiles and deceives the

lady, while Petrarch loves with sincere, immutable devotion. Petrarch and Donne similarly treat the sun as a kind of " gaita," the third character participating in the *alba*, who at one time functions as a watchman or guard warning the lovers when they must part, and at others as a rival or an intruder.[5]

Donne's lover in " The Sunne Rising " also views the sun as an intruder. As in the medieval *alba*, Donne rages against the " gaita " for disturbing the night of love. He flaunts the power of his love, boasting that he could " eclipse and cloud " the sun's proverbially reverend beams. The heroic *vanto* is a way of deprecating his rival while affirming that inspired by the ennoblement of love, a lover can achieve any knightly feat, even that of conquering nature's most powerful force. In Donne's poem the lover tries to convince the sun of the superiority of his beloved and their ideal world of love over the real world, while in Petrarch's sonnet CXV the sun seems already aware of this fact, and is now intent on actually winning the lady away from the human rival. In Petrarch's poem the sun not only symbolizes life-giving warmth and energy, but more importantly it is a symbol of divinity, and significantly the human lover wins out over the divine sun.

The sun as divinity[6] is retained in " The Sunne Rising," but Donne extends the implications of the symbol. It is not only a question of the human conquering the divine as in Petrarch, but more of the human possessing and incorporating the divine within his microcosm. The speaker, reminding the sun that nothing in the world is real except their love, quips,

> Thine age askes ease, and since thy duties bee
> To warme the world, that's done in warming us.

The speaker's obsessive attempt to win the sun over to his way of thinking suggests his implicit desire to achieve immortality by becoming divine through love. He recognizes that love is conditioned by the arrival of daylight and the claims of the real world. If the sun, the symbol of eternal life, can be incorporated into the lovers' world, then immortality has become a reality. The lover's argument with the sun suggests his awareness that the claims of self-sufficiency are contingent upon enlisting the sun's aid. He remarks,

> Love, all alike, no season knowes, nor clyme,
> Nor houres, dayes, months, which are the rags of time.

Theoretically, the ideal claims of Petrarchan love, that it is immutable and eternal are true, but in practice the lover knows that they are true only if the sun, the marker of changing time, can be enlisted to serve only the lovers.

Petrarch expresses a similar idea in sonnet CLXXXVIII in which he directly implores the sun, whom Petrarch refers to as Laura's first lover, to retard his motions and thus not deny him the grace of his lady's image, " ove favilla il mio soave foco."

> Almo Sol, quella fronde ch'io sola amo,
> tu prima amasti, or sola al bel soggiorno
> verdeggia, et senza par poi che l'addorno
> suo male et nostro vide in prima Adamo.
>
> Stiamo a mirarla; i' ti pur prego et chiamo,
> o Sole; et tu pur fuggi, et fai d'intorno
> ombrare i poggi, et te ne porti il giorno,
> et fuggendo mi toi quel ch'i' piú bramo.
>
> L'ombra che cade da quel'humil colle,
> ove favilla il mio soave foco,
> ove 'l gran lauro fu picciola verga,
>
> crescendo mentr'io parlo, agli occhi tolle
> la dolce vista del beato loco,
> ove 'l mio cor co la sua donna alberga.

The images of the lady and the sun in this sonnet are ambivalent. At first Laura is silently compared to the laurel, an allegorical reference to Apollo's love for Daphne, but we know that the Sun-God's affections were far from monogamous or consistent. The sun's motions are responsible for the arrival of winter, a season Petrarch laments as not conducive to love. Laura is associated with spring, the symbol of perpetual renewal and hopeful anticipation, and her growing, maturing beauty is unequalled in the history of mankind. These positive associations are suddenly undercut by Petrarch's metaphorical paralleling of Laura to Eve, the " adorno male." Moreover, the sun, in marking the passage of each day with subsequent night, not only regularly denies the lover his life-giving vision, but also causes the vicissitudes of age to be felt by his lady whom he remembers at one time " fu picciola verga."

Donne's lover is likewise aware of the vicissitudes threatening love, perhaps the " sharpe Norths and declining Wests " mentioned in " The Good-morrow," and the fact that love abides in its own microcosm does not protect it from these vicissitudes. The lover's challenge to the sun is motivated by his awareness, like Petrarch's, that love *does* have " seasons." Whether the sun reserves his warming and life-giving services exclusively for the lovers' world or not, he will still retain his characteristic duty as the marker of passing time, and in this sense the sun's power here, as in Petrarch's sonnet, is ambivalent. Petrarch and Donne's lover cannot escape the reality that their amorous microcosms must exist within a larger world of time. Conspicuously, their dawn-dialogues with the sun are all one-sided; the sun concedes no response, nor do we, or the lovers, for that matter, expect any. They have voiced the feelings of exclusiveness and the desire for permanence which all lovers experience, especially as in " The Sunne Rising," during their moments of fulfilled love. Secretly they know that this is the closest man can come to eternity and immutability in this life.

The image of the amorous microcosm and the relationship of the sun to that microcosm exemplifies how Donne attempted to adjust an ideal conception of love to the inescapable claims of the real world. The lovers' world in " The Sunne Rising " is an ideal construct of sexual fulfillment and spiritual contemplation; it reconciles the fanciful dreams and hopes of Petrarch's somewhat romantically pure ideal with the frankly sensual gratification of the Ovidian conception of love; it combines adoration and possession, time and eternity.

" The Sunne Rising " tries to resolve the inherent problems of an unrequited love which the Petrarchan motifs dramatize by affirming that the ideal love is one that is mutual, one that can exist within the context of the demands of a real world. The ideals of Petrarchan love prevail in the poem relatively unchanged, while Donne's uniqueness resides in his explicit rendering of new associations or combinations between the ideal and real worlds which do not appear in Petrarch. In doing so, Donne paradoxically offers a view of love which in some ways is even more " ideal " and unconventional than Petrarch's, for Donne in this poem refuses to accept, as Petrarch does, earthly love's ultimate subjection to time.

VI. PETRARCHAN IMAGERY
IN " THE CANONIZATION "

The story of English Renaissance literature is to a large extent one of how the writers of this remarkable literary period relate to or were influenced by the traditions and developments of Italian literature. Perhaps the most pervasive Italian force operating in English Renaissance literature is Petrarchism, and whereas it has been claimed that the most original and innovative English writers were those who rebelled against it to assert their native or personal impulses, gradually the important, positive contribution of the Petrarchan love ethic and style in the development of English love poetry is now being recognized. Petrarch provided the Renaissance love poets with an elaborate dictionary of amorous terminology and a rhetorical handbook of poetic devices which they undoubtedly could not ignore or escape despite their own national or personal inclinations. The relationship of poets like Spenser, Shakespeare, Sidney, and Donne to Petrarch and to the tradition which bears his name is much more complex than may have been previously thought. In the case of Donne, who has been praised for his so-called rejection of overused Petrarchan elements, his originality may indeed lie not in the denial of a tradition, but rather in its adaptation and subtle assimilation.

A careful tracing of the labyrinthian ways in which Petrarchism affected the course of English Renaissance literature often leads to interesting discoveries and modified judgments. D.D. Carnicelli's *Lord Morley's Tryumphes of Fraunces Petrarcke* (Cambridge, Mass., 1971) offers a much needed inquiry into a side of Renaissance Petrarchism too long neglected by demonstrating how interest in Petrarch's *Trionfi*, less known, of course, than the obviously influential *Canzoniere*, significantly affected the development of English Renaissance literature. Although, as Carnicelli says, " ... no appreciable body of poetry comparable to the sonnet sequences generated by the *Canzoniere* seems to have been inspired by the *Trionfi* " (p. 27), the indirect influence of this disregarded aspect of Petrarchism may extend to seemingly unlikely works such as Donne's *Anniversaries*, for example, whose meaning, method, and effect may be further clarified by viewing them within the *triumph* tradition. The value of a more sophisticated and comprehensive definition and application of Petrarchism is evident, yet one need not strain for exotic comparative studies, since new insights can be gleaned from a less provincial re-evaluation of familiar works in terms of how they relate to literary precedents and traditions. By uncovering places where the English Renaissance poets employed Petrarchan analogues openly or where they used their implications as camouflaged subsurface scaffolding, we can more accurately determine to what extend and in what manner they were innovative. Donne's transformation of Petrarchan imagery in " The Canonization " offers a specific instance of how Petrarchan analogues function in his poetry and how they contribute to its ultimately original effect.

" The Canonization " is undoubtedly one of Donne's most unique yet most conventional poems. Donne's originality here, and often elsewhere in the *Songs and Sonnets*, resides not so much in his realistic portrayal of love, but rather in his skillful manipulation and synthesis of Petrarchan images and themes. The Petrarchan sources for the images in stanza two of the poem—the sighs, tear-floods, colds, heats, etc.—have been noted and for the most part analyzed in terms of how Donne adapts them to his poetic context.[1] Some of the Petrarchan analogues for the images in stanza three have been acknowledged; [2] yet others have remained unnoticed, while the implications of the cross-references have been generally ignored or unexplored. A clearer understanding of both Donne's originality and conventionality requires not only a citation of analogues, but also a demonstration of how Donne specifically relates to those sources, how he varies them, for what purpose, and to what ultimate effect in his poetry. This essay will attempt to develop the relationship of neglected and, in some cases, already cited Petrarchan analogues to the imagery Donne uses in the third

stanza of " The Canonization " in order to show how the function of the images in Petrarch is similar to or different from
that in Donne.

Donne's use of the images of the fly-taper, eagle, and
phoenix in the third stanza is informed by Petrarch's use of
similar images in the *Canzoniere*.[3] For example, sonnet XIX,
" Son animali al mondo de sì altera," provides an illuminating
context for Donne's use of the fly-taper image:

> Son animali al mondo de sí altera
> vista che 'ncontra 'l sol pur si difende;
> altri, però che 'l gran lume gli offende,
> non escon fuor se non verso la sera;
>
> et altri, col desio folle che spera
> gioir forse nel foco, perché splende,
> provan l'altra vertú, quella che 'ncende:
> lasso, e 'l mio loco è 'n questa ultima schera.
>
> Ch'i' non son forte ad aspectar la luce
> di questa donna, et non so fare schermi
> di luoghi tenebrosi, o d'ore tarde:
>
> però con gli occhi lagrimosi e 'nfermi
> mio destino a vederla mi conduce;
> et so ben ch'i' vo dietro a quel che m'arde.

Petrarch catalogues three types of flying creatures according to
the way in which they react to light—an obvious metaphor for
the love he believes embodied in and emanating from his lady.
The first is the proud eagle which soaring into the sky stares
at the sun without any noticeable damage—" che 'ncontra 'l
sol pur si difende." The second is the owl, which aware of the
danger, comes out only under the protection of the night. The
third, butterflies, moths, flies, and the like possess a suicidal
desire (" desio folle ") to seek the fiery sun's rays, which in-
flict inevitable death. The sunlight is implicitly compared to
the light of a candle's taper whose deadly beauty attracts the
fly. Petrarch considers himself a member of this third group—" e
'l mio loco è 'n questa ultima schera." [5] He lacks the daring
strength of the eagle and the clever caution of the night birds.
Like the moth, he consumes himself with passion.

Another analogue for Donne's use of the fly-taper image
is sonnet CXLI, in which Petrarch compares himself to a butterfly, who coming out at night and unaccustomed to darkness,
inadvertently flies into the attracting eyes of people who cause
its death. Similarly Petrarch is irrationally and compulsively
drawn to the fatal light emanating from Laura's eyes:

> Come talora al caldo tempo sòle
> semplicetta farfalla al lume avezza
> volar negli occhi altrui per sua vaghezza,
> onde aven ch'ella more, altri si dole.

The butterfly personifies the repudiated and unreasoning lover,
whose soul in yielding to the uncontrolled desires of the sensual
appetite suffers death:

> cosí sempre io corro al fatal mio sole
> degli occhi onde mi vèn tanta dolcezza
> che 'l fren de la ragion Amor non prezza,
> e chi discerne è vinto da chi vòle.

> E veggio ben quant'elli a schivo m'ànno,
> e so ch'i' ne morrò veracemente,
> ché mia vertú non pò contra l'affanno;

> ma sí m'abbaglia Amor soavemente,
> ch'i' piango l'altrui noia, et no 'l mio danno;
> et cieca al suo morir l'alma consente.

In both sonnets XIX and CXLI Petrarch is fully aware of the
self-annihilating consequences of his passion, but vows to persist
in his love anyway. His obstinacy is similar to Donne's assertion
in " The Canonization " to love " and at our own cost die."
Thus, Petrarch uses the fly-taper image negatively to point out
his inability to transcend the destructive sexual desire which
subsists in his devotion to Laura.

In " The Canonization " the fly-taper image suggests on
the surface the self-destructive nature of Petrarchan love, in
addition to the ephemerality which the lover recognizes as
characteristic of everything else in the world except their love.
In the first stanza with his allusions to " palsie," gout, gray hair,
fortune, wealth, etc., the speaker has shown that he is aware

of the imperfection, instability, and transiency, of the earthly condition in which love must abide, but the images in stanza three support his belief that real love will transcend fleeting sexual pleasure and earthly vicissitude. Lines 19-22 indicate that the friend addressed in the poem, who presumably has criticized love, has characterized it as suicidal, recalling Petrarch's " desio folle." [6] The speaker in defending himself first makes the friend's accusation more plausible by citing the fly-taper image and by pretending to accept his friend's claim; but his acceptance is only a temporary ploy, for he uses the image not, as in Petrarch, isolated from any other considerations about the love. The image in Donne functions as the basis of an elaborate defense the speaker builds to assert the exclusive nature of his love and how it differs from an irrational, unstable Petrarchan love whose evil effects are grief and self-destruction. The speaker's ultimate goal is to prove that the love, although temporarily self-consuming, is not irreparably self-annihilating, because it does not remain on a physical level.

Donne's use of the well-known phoenix image (1.23) is similarly informed by Petrarch's use of the same image. However, the purpose differs in the two poets, since in Petrarch the phoenix symbolizes the hopeless cyclical pattern of his thwarted love, while in Donne the image expresses how the lovers transcend the immediately deadening physical effects of their consummated love.[7] In canzone CXXXV, " Qual più diversa et nova," Petrarch describes the many miraculous transformations he claims to have undergone through love, but the metamorphoses are neither welcomed nor desired, for they merely indicate the unthriving and arrested nature of his love. Petrarch employs the phoenix analogy, and the subsequent images of the stone, beast, and fountain, to heighten dramatically the extraordinary unhappiness and anxiety resulting from his ill-fated love:

> Qual piú diversa et nova
> cosa fu mai in qual che stranio clima,
> quella, se ben s'estima,
> piú mi rasembra: a tal son giunto, Amore.
> Là onde il dí vèn fore,

> vola un augel che sol senza consorte
> di volontaria morte
> rinasce, et tutto a viver si rinova.
> Cosí sol si ritrova
> lo mio voler, et cosí in su la cima
> de' suoi alti pensieri al sol si volve,
> et cosí si risolve,
> et cosí torna al suo stato di prima:
> arde, et more, et riprende i nervi suoi,
> et vive poi con la fenice a prova.

The resurrection of the phoenix, rather than suggesting perpetual life, is here viewed as a condemnation for Petrarch. He sees himself as a second phoenix figuratively re-enacting the legendary ritual which perpetuates his amorous pains.[8]

Unlike Petrarch who portrays himself as an isolated phoenix locked in a repetitive pattern of futile suffering, Donne's use of the image in " The Canonization " projects the mutual love which allows the lovers to " dye and rise the same, and prove/Mysterious by this love." Both lovers in Donne simultaneously experience the miracle of the phoenix and are transformed by it into " one neutral thing." Their metamorphosis has rendered them paradoxically immutable and above carnality.

The function of the images in stanza three has been to disprove the argument that love is impermanent and self-destructive by reapplying the conventional analogies which project such a claim in the Petrarchan context to an alternate interpretation of love's nature and effects. The apparent shift in tone and imagery from the second to the third stanza indicates a shift from the physical to the supra-lunary world of the lovers in preparation for his definition of love as an unprecedented synthesis of sensual and spiritual, immune to vicissitude. Stanzas four and five then assert love's permanence and ennobling effects through the variation of two additional Petrarchan claims: art will immortalize their devotion much in the same way that religious hymns immortalize the miracles of saints, and the world's subsequent lovers assure them fame by using them as paragons for imitation.[9] Donne's romantic and idealized solution to physical ephemerality, as reflected by his transformation of Petrarchan imagery, in some respects exceeds Petrarch's idealization. Far from the realism for which he has so often been praised, Donne's love here is mutual, rational, transcendental, and confidently self-immortalizing. While Petrarch strives for and glorifies this ideal, he remains victim to a hopeless love—unrequited, irrational, sensual, and obstinately self-destructive.

Yet Donne's memorable defense in support of an idealized view of love, like so many others in Renaissance love poetry, finds its model in Petrarch who more than anyone was responsible for its popularity and poetic eternalization. Ugo Foscolo's lines epitomize well both the essential nature of Petrarchism and the reason why Renaissance artists, so intent on aspiring toward the ideal, were attracted to the potential sublimity inherent if not actualized in Petrarch's love ethic and directly or indirectly reflect it in their own statements:

> E tu i cari parenti e l'idioma
> Desti a quel dolce di Calliope labbro
> Che amore in Grecia nudo e nudo in Roma
> D'un velo candidissimo adornando,
> Rendea nel grembo a Venere Celeste.[10]

VII. FOOLS, HEROES, AND SAINTS: THE PETRARCHAN HOPE FOR FAME

The love experience, whether mutual or unrequited, ultimately leads to a questioning of its permanence in this life and its possible extension in the life hereafter. The lover may believe that the love will endure despite the inescapable claims of earthly vicissitude because it is a perfect balance of physical and spiritual, or that it will endure after the lovers die because it will continue to exert influence in the earthly sphere. The fame theme as it appears in Petrarch's love poetry deals mostly with the second kind of permanence—his desire to make some indelible mark on this world to assure that all was not in vain. By *fame* is meant the way the lover views his love in relation to present and future worldly opinion. The desire for fame indicates an awareness of man's limitations and of the inadequacies of earthly love, no matter how humanly perfect. In the *Canzoniere* Petrarch desires to achieve divine stability and absoluteness through the immortality of the written word. He aspires to permanence through love and poetry because he is dissatisfied with the ineffable and precarious nature of all that is earthly. The hope for present and future worldly recognition exposes his aspiration to conquer the relativity of this existence.

The fame theme in the *Canzoniere* takes the form of the search, through amorous poetry, for artistic recognition and glory during and after Petrarch's lifetime. Although Petrarch claims he writes in order to immortalize his lady, he really seeks self-glorification through literary art, "... la sopravvivenza del suo nome nelle età venture." [1] This intention, revealed throughout the *Canzoniere*, is conspicuously and honestly admitted at the end of canzone LXXI, one of the three famous exaltations of Laura's eyes:

> onde parole et opre
> escon di me sí fatte allor ch' i' spero
> farmi immortal, perché la carne moia.

The *Canzoniere* as a whole dramatizes the relationship of love, human and divine, to the writing of good poetry, and how both will fulfill Petrarch's aspirations for fame.

Petrarch's apparently self-serving wish for glory derives from his unreciprocated love. He gradually sublimates his frustrated but unrelenting desire for Laura's acceptance, and begins to think in terms of literary recognition and acceptance, though at times even this seems remote. The quest for the poetic *laurea* becomes easier once Laura is dead, since his energies and talents are no longer distracted by the obsessive but veiled wish for sexual gratification. Often he asserts that his task is to perpetuate Laura's memory on earth through his poetry:

> Et sua fama, che spira
> in molte parti anchor per la tua lingua,
> prega che non extingua,
> anzi la voce al suo nome rischiari.
>
> -CCLXVIII

He even rationalizes her disdain of his love during her lifetime by saying that it helped him to cultivate virtue and to perfect his art, which in turn will lead him to acquire fame and glory:

> O leggiadre arti et lor effetti degni,
> l'un co la lingua oprar, l'altra col ciglio,
> io gloria in lei, et ella in me virtute!
>
> -CCLXXXIX

Yet Petrarch has substituted one idolatrous devotion for another, and despite his claim in the sonnets in death that he is writing about a better love, a sacred love, his constant concern about the importance of effective rhetoric in gaining worldly fame reveals self-love posing as dedication to others.

Petrarchan love, then, is shown to foster a total usurpation of the poet-lover's heart and artistic talent, while encouraging an obsessive concern for earthly fame. The lover devotes his art to human love—mostly love of self—from which he hopes to gain immortality, not in the kingdom of God, but on this earth.

Donne's *Songs and Sonnets* have much in common with the overall attitude toward fame described as characteristic of Petrarch's sequence. Donne is not, like Petrarch, obsessively concerned, at least not consciously, with seeking immortal self-glorification through love poetry. However, in several poems he adapts the Petrarchan fame theme to portray his own unique vision of man's quest for permanence through mutual love and the written word. Although there are some Petrarchan ideas on fame which Donne does not consider in the *Songs*,[2] there are others which he accepts with little modification of thought, but which he creatively adjusts to his own view of love. The dominant attitude toward fame revealed in the *Songs* is, in fact, determined by Donne's concept of reciprocated love, just as Petrarch's treatment of fame derives from his picture of thwarted love. When Donne's speaker is a denied Petrarchan lover, then, like Petrarch, he sees poetry as a vent for amorous frustration, and fame as a substitute for the acceptance and fulfillment refused him. Dissatisfaction with the earthly love relationship causes the lover to seek eternal self-glorification, which is his way of improving an otherwise unrewarding, incomplete human relationship. But when he is a mutual lover, his desire for fame reflects his need to eternalize fleeting joy and to communicate or share his happiness with the rest of the world. Mutual lovers, such as those in Donne's " The Sunne Rising " and " The Canonization," see themselves as paragons of human love, and the greatest recognition they can receive is the flattery of imitation. Their own self-congratulation is a weak substitute for worldy fame. Both attitudes toward fame indicate the lover's need to make a permanent imprint on this world before he and his lady pass on to uncertainty. Concern about their reputations once dead and their wish for eternal recognition are aspects of the desire to transcend time and bodily decay. Lovers may say that they are otherworldly, but why do they seek, in Donne's words, " to anger destiny " by desiring fame?

Donne's speakers seem as intent as Petrarch on immortalizing themselves and their love. In both poets the wish for fame reveals an awareness of the limitations of the amorous microcosm when compared to the apparent indestructability of the macrocosm. The lover sees that his world of love, no matter how humanly perfect, eventually succumbs to the force of death, while the seemingly decay-ridden macrocosm prevails. Donne's speakers cherish the idea of exclusiveness which underlies the Petrarchan theme of fame, and they adhere to the assumption that the only way to assure the permanent survival of love is through the enduring memorial which poetry offers. Although Donne's *Songs* confirm many Petrarchan ideas on fame, it is the way he reshapes them to his own vision of mutual love which accounts for their original quality.

In " The Triple Foole " the speaker re-examines the claim of the essential relationship between love and poetry basic to the *Canzoniere*. This claim is reflected in canzone CXXV, which turns on the notion of Petrarch's desire to poetize the passion of his heart, in the hope that his art will cause the lady to return his love:

> Se 'l pensier che mi strugge,
> com'è pungente et saldo,
> cosí vestisse d'un color conforme,
> forse tal m'arde et fugge,
> ch'avria parte del caldo,
> et desteriasi Amor là dov'or dorme.

The opening lines of canzone CXXVII reassert his need to vent his long suffering passion through " le dogliose rime," concluding that his "... sospiri/parlando 'an triegua, et al dolor soccorro." In sonnet LXXIV Petrarch admits that he has wasted much ink and paper on his lady's account:

> et ché pie' miei non son fiaccati et lassi
> a seguir l'orme vostre in ogni parte
> perdendo inutilmente tanti passi;

> et onde vien l'enchiostro, onde le carte
> ch'i' vo empiendo di voi: se n' ciò fallassi,
> colpa d'Amor, non già defecto d'arte.

Canzone CCXXXIX concedes his artistic failure in moving Laura to love him and acknowledges the foolish vanity of further attempts:

> Ma pria fia 'l verno la stagion de' fiori,
> ch'amor fiorisca in quella nobil alma,
> che non curò già mai rime né versi.
>
> Quante lagrime, lasso, et quanti versi
> ò già sparti al mio tempo, e 'n quante note
> ò riprovato humilïar quell'alma!

The extent of Donne's originality in " The Triple Foole " is more clearly evaluated by the knowledge that he assimilates and elaborates Petrarchan motifs while adding a surface gaiety and casualness to the speaker's attitude of self-blame—qualities never present in Petrarch's austere treatment of the subject. Yet in the manner of Petrarch's canzone CCXXXIX, Donne's speaker, who identifies himself as at least formerly a Petrarchan poet-lover, derogates his love and his poetry, for he is foolish to love a lady who denies him, and doubly foolish for writing about it:

> I am two fooles, I know,
> For loving, and for saying so
> In whining Poetry.

In lines 4-5 he admits that his love is unrequited and that he initially had turned to poetry with the Petrarchan hope that his pain and grief would be allayed " through Rimes vexation," just as the earth's rivers and streams " purge sea waters fretful salt away." By externalizing his grief and disciplining it into a poetic form, he had hoped, like Petrarch, to relieve his anguish. But unfortunately the process was not allowed to stop there, and, thus, the valuable effect of poetry as a means of venting amorous grief is undermined. A song writer who came across

the lyrics decided to put the poems to music, which resulted
in a renewing and increasing of the poet-lover's affliction as
the amoorous emotions were released from their restraining
form. Thus, the Petrarchan idea was not adhered to exactly.
The speaker may have been wise in following its original dictates, but its good effects were superseded by allowing the grief
to be put to music. If the reading of verse devoted to love's
grief gives pleasure, then it will increase the lover's pain because
by such verse " their triumphs so are published." The speaker
is a " triple foole " to the world, for he failed to conceal the
foolishness of his unrequited love. So while the Petrarchan
lover is driven by the need for psychological release, he cannot
yield to this need for fear of the world's ridicule.

In comparing Donne's treatment of the fame theme in
this poem to Petrarch's we find that Donne's approach is
typically more light-hearted and less self-pitying; he is more
resigned to what he has discovered are the cruel lessons of
love. Donne dramatizes the fame theme by adding a super-
structure of elaborate narrative details. By means of this fiction
Donne shows how the Petrarchan idea of venting amorous
emotions, when applied or redefined in the context of a realistic
situation and carried beyond the limitations of an idealized
world, can be ultimately ineffective if not useless. But what is
significantly original about Donne's approach is that it subtly
accentuates the conventional image of the suffering Petrarchan
lover by showing how in this speaker's case the fame his love
experience received (by putting poetry to music) merely in-
creased his amorous grief.

" The Undertaking," a somewhat neglected poem, explores
the fame theme in an interesting and unexpected way. An
implicit tension is set up between the " heroic " context within
which the speaker sees himself and the " secret " love which
he says has caused his heroism. As in other poems where
parody is the central device, here Donne parodies the conventional image of the discreet, idealizing Petrarchan lover by
paralleling him to the epic hero. The qualities of the speaker
and of his " brave undertaking " are variations of characteristics
found in Petrarch and in the courtly code. Love must be kept

secret from profane men who will ridicule and destroy it. The lover must concentrate on the lady's virtue, the " lovelinesse within," for her physical beauty is never an end in itself, but a reflection of her inner spiritual beauty, which will abide once the outer beauty has changed and decayed. Viewing his love as unique, exclusive, and aristocratic, the Petrarchan lover in " The Undertaking " sees only " vertue attir'd," forgetting the " Hee and Shee." The thrust of the speaker's description in stanzas four and five points to the permanence of this kind of love in the face of inevitable physical decay, while its rarity supports his call for secrecy.

But his expressed desire for secrecy and his self-acknow-ledged exclusiveness are ironic since he voices his sighs in poetry which unveils his private " undertaking " to the scrutiny of all men, aristocratic and common. It would seem that this speaker is driven by the same need for expression as the speaker of " The Triple Foole." In fact, the poem is a boast, or *vanto*, a poetic form common in an heroic context, and what he im-plicitly seeks to have recognized and rewarded is his idealized love. He portrays himself paradoxically as a " hero " of Petrarchan love, and the musical quality of the poem's rhythm reinforces its relationship to the oral tradition of the epic, whose purpose was to sing of the feats of an Achilles or of a Roland. His self-description is in terms of the heroic deeds of such " Worthies," but the difference between this hero and past figures is that he wants to keep his undertaking hidden, or at least so he claims. The confusion between the speaker's self-image and the kind of love he purports as responsible for this image leads us to discount that he has fully committed himself to the Petrarchan ideal. The speaker of " The Under-taking " wants the best of both worlds, for although he says he espouses the idealism of Petrarchan love, he reveals himself as unable to abide by its most important rule—secrecy. The validity of his call for secrecy is further undermined by his implicit directive for imitation by the masses. True to the idea which sees the hero as a paragon, the speaker considers himself a model for emulation by all " brave " lovers, whose imitation assures him fame and supplies him with the reward all good heroes should receive. But his desire for recognition, that he has " done a braver thing/ Then all the Worthies did," indicates that he has not really espoused Petrarchan love at all. The speaker of " The Undertaking " needs self-identification, and ironically he seeks it in terms of the heroic feat he says he has accomplished. The call for imitation seems to contradict his previous call for secrecy. One reason the lover might want to keep the love secret is because, as in " The Triple Foole," he is actually ashamed of his unrequited Petrarchan passion. Mutual lovers are always ready to flaunt their love. The speaker's unconscious feelings in " The Undertaking " can be compared to Petrarch's sonnet XXXV in which he seeks solitude and isolation from people, who he imagines will mock him when they discover he loves a denying lady. The irony of Petrarch's quest for protective isolation is that no matter where he journies, Love seems to be his ever-constant companion. But as a whole, Donne's treatment of the fame theme in " The Undertaking " seems to defy specific parallelism with Petrarchan analogues.

Through the fame theme the heroic idea of love as conquest and the idealized view of love as courtship converge and are redefined in " The Undertaking." The speaker's attitude toward recognition and reward is ambiguous, for while in one breath he says that it is " braver... to keep that hid," in another he offers himself as a paragon. He compares his spiritualized and passive love with the externalized and active feats of warriors, asserting that *his* heroism is even greater because he has maintained secrecy. But has he?

In " The Relique " the speaker muses about what will happen when after his death someone digs up the lovers' grave, for as mutual lovers he foresees that he and his lady will be buried together. The lovers are mutual but unrequited, since their relationship as described in stanza three seems to exclude sex. The poem is a variation of two ideas in Petrarch—in one the lover imagines that he will join his lady after death, and in the other he projects what people will think and say about him once dead. Sonnets CCLXXVIII, CCCXIII, CCCXLIX offer significant examples. Petrarch's characteristic imaginings about his post-mortem state suggest his desire for external recognition and reward. His impossible quest for a perfect love in this life leads him to call on death, finally allowing him to join his beloved, but not without the fame he hopes his poetry will bring. Thus, in Petrarch literary immortality is a reward for the lover's sacrificing devotion.[3]

Donne enlarges the scope of both motifs by treating them within the context of a fictional hypothesis he constructs to examine not only the lover's obsessive concern for recognition and fame, but also the very nature and possibility of Petrarchan love. The fictional quality of the poem's content is stressed by the speaker's use of the word " when " to begin stanza one and " if " to begin stanza two. Although the story he tells is vivid and realistic, the hypothetical nature of his conclusions qualifies their validity. The description of an idealistic and miraculous Petrarchan love is undercut not only by the flippant tone carried throughout, but also by the use of certain allusions, such as that comparing the lady to Mary Magdalen, remembered as a great profane lover before she ever became a saint. Donne, like Petrarch, compares his lady to a Mary, but for Petrarch it is the Virgin Mary. Moreover, the improbability of the episode described in " The Relique " coupled with the suggestion in the poem's last lines of the impossibility of such a " miraculous " love imply that it would rarely find adequate justification in reality. Using the dramatic death-scene context reinforced by Petrarchan motifs, Donne again presents a parody in the sense both of a burlesque and an imitation, of those who advocate the miracles of " harmless lovers " and who expect a reward for their sacrifice.

The poem's graveyard setting dramatizes the importance of the essential relationship between the living and the dead in the lover's attempt to secure fame. The poem itself does not portray the inevitability of decay and death, but they are assumed as inescapable facts. Fame is viewed as the only stable force in an otherwise constantly changing universe, and the relic—the " bracelet of bright haire about the bone "—symbolizes the lovers' permanence in the face of decay and death.

Acting as an eternal objectification, or extension, of their love, the relic will commemorate to posterity their devotion, just as the love-poem immortalizes love. As tangible evidence of their love, it assures that some lasting part of themselves and their love will survive and perhaps influence future generations. The significance of the relationship between the living and the dead is embodied in the survival and recovery of the relic. The lover's concern with their posthumous influence on posterity is ironic, however, for while alive lovers commonly seek to isolate themselves from the common world. They pride themselves in the knowledge that their microcosm is isolated from and even immune to the macrocosmic vicissitudes. But after death, as in " The Relique," the lover imagines the effect of their love on posterity in terms of how people will respond to the discovery of their relic. The bracelet is not only a symbol of their eternal love and companionship, but it also serves as a link between them and future generations. It assures the lovers continuity despite their personal obliteration.

In the first stanza posterity's judgment of the lovers is represented by the individual figure of the gravedigger who will presumably imagine that the bracelet was a " devise.../ To make their soules at the last busie day,/ Meet at this grave, and make a little stay." His is a purely secular response, assuring only a " secular " fame. In the second stanza posterity's judgment assumes a more religious, or idolatrous character. A superstitious age of misdevotion will confer fame on the lovers by turning them into pseudosaints, and consistent with the influence of saints, the speaker imagines that their fame will be enhanced by the legend surrounding them, " I would that age were by their paper taught/ What miracle wee harmlesse lovers wrought." The final stanza explains why they will achieve fame because of the kind of love that passes between them. Although the physical is not excluded totally from their relationship, for the lovers do kiss, their love is generally restrained, miraculous (and miracles are always assured fame), first, because the lovers " knew not what wee lov'd, nor why," and second, they knew no " difference of sex," and last, they had not broken the " seales " of nature. It would seem, then, that the speaker equates fame and sainthood, saying that the lovers' transformation into saints is achieved because they resisted the temptations of the flesh. At the end the speaker reveals that the greatest " miracle " of all was the lady, and with this exalting compliment we realize that the love described is Petrarchan.

With this revelation we conclude that this Petrarchan lover, like Petrarch himself, sees fame as a substitute for the lack of sexual fulfillment in his earthly love, and the obvious ambiguity of his statements about women and chastity (11, 3-4, 17-18, 28-30) becomes clearer. These statements show the inability to hide his sexual frustration, even though he may be sincerely espousing a " purer " kind of love. The use of religious images and language is the speaker's way of camouflaging his sexual desires. Moreover, the speaker's desire for fame is not only an attempt to mitigate his sexual deprivation, but it also reveals his implicit fear of death and his hope for continuity, which the relic seems to assure. Yet the relic itself is questionable in its meaning. The erotic implications of the camouflaged images and language may suggest an erotic meaning for the relic as well, in which case the relic is not only a symbol immortalizing their idealistic love, but it is also a projection of the speaker's unfulfilled desires which he sees in some perverse way being satisfied in the after-life—a kind of post-mortem sexual wish-fulfillment.

Donne's treatment of the fame theme here is different from Petrarch's lamenting sighs and sand-castle hopes. Donne is more dramatic, more realistic, more vivid. In " The Relique " Petrarchan notions are merely catalysts for Donne's own witty response to a woman who insists on at least the appearance of a " saintly " kind of love. Yet the core ideas are the same—the post-mortem imaginings, the hope for immortality either by poems or relics, the desire for fame as a compensating substitute for sexual deprivation.

In " The Triple Foole," " The Undertaking," and " The Relique " we see how Donne skillfully molds Petrarchan ideas

to his own creative purposes. At times he follows the Petrarchan
analogue, while more often it is merely a springboard for his
own witty, innovative, and dramatic variation. Yet in both
cases recognition of the Petrarchan ideas and devices which
often are at the heart of his love poems allows us to determine
more clearly to what extent Donne was in fact a revolutionary
poet.

VIII. DONNE'S IRONIC REVERSAL
OF PETRARCHAN DEATH MOTIFS

I have been showing how Donne's love poetry is thrown into an interesting light when studied in direct comparison with Petrarch's portrayal of similar themes and situations in the *Canzoniere*. In addition to offering alternate readings of Donne's poetry, a direct comparative study has revealed that Donne assimilated and utilized Petrarchan ideals and themes in a witty, humorous, and inventive way, and rather than rebelling against it, as was thought by older critics, he was able to express himself creatively within the conventional limits of Petrarchanism.[1] In fact, it is in Donne's transmutation of Petrarchan themes and imagery that he makes his most original contribution to the literary tradition of love poetry. A direct comparison between Petrarch's treatment of death in the *Canzoniere* and Donne's in the *Songs* offers a pertinent example of the extent to which Donne absorbed and transformed Petrarchan aspects in an original way. Such a comparison does not mean that Donne was directly influenced by Petrarch or that he was consciously imitating or rebelling against him. Instead it points out how pervasive the so-called " Petrarchan mode " was and how useful it could be to poets such as Donne who later were praised for their uniqueness and originality.

The Petrarchan lover is not always consoled as he sometimes is by the imagined success of triumphing over death through the permanence of the written word. The Petrarchan motif of literary fame substituting for sexual fulfillment is in turn replaced by another—death as the inescapable physical effect of obsessive human love. This realization is especially evident when Petrarch is faced with the event of his beloved's death, or when his unrequited state forces him to experience the paradoxical living-death (" viva morte ") of amorous denial.

The story of his love is often marked by the occurrence of three kinds of death: the lover's figurative death caused by unfulfilled passion, the lady's death following a disease, and the lover's figurative and literal death produced by the loss of his beloved. Whichever experience of death the lover faces, it governs his attitude toward the rest of the world. For example, the perversity of unrequited love resulting from the lady's denial reflects to him the deprivation and perversity of the world as a whole. He judges the world, his relationship to it and to posterity, in terms of himself or of his loss. Death is sometimes viewed as a method for taking revenge on love, on the lady, or on the world itself. At other times, as when he faces the death of his lady, his personal demise offers him the possibility of relief from suffering. She is unquestionably responsible for his life and death, both figuratively and literally, for she is the spirit that animates his microcosm and the macrocosm, and her loss, whether it be in the form of sexual denial, absence, or physical death, results in a disintegration within and outside the lover.

Donne's *Songs* on death are marked by the repetitive yet transformed use of Petrarchan *topos* as the lover struggles to come to terms with an uncontrollable force. Pretense and wishful thinking subsist beneath the lover's threats employed as emotional blackmail or as a weak method of staying the encroachment of old age and literal death, or the death by castration caused by a denying female. The motif of the living-death coupled with that of the lover as death's powerless victim offer a grim picture of his inability to transcend the desires of the flesh and the mortal claims of this earth. The use of religious imagery to veil the sexual overtones, successful in other amorous contingencies, here functions neither to ennoble the love nor to offer hope, but merely intensifies the lover's inability to conquer death, heightens his grief, fear, and despair, and confirms his cynical pessimism. And perhaps more than anything else, the distinct separation between lover and beloved, the absolute sense of alienation and isolation, the lack of oneness and of the hope for unity, most characterize Donne's treatment of the Petrarchan theme of death in the *Songs and Sonnets.*

" The Will," " The Funerall," and " The Dampe " are poems on the lover's death resulting from unrequited passion. The speaker of " The Will " is a disillusioned Petrarchan lover who views idealistic but unfulfilled love as cruel and perverse. Its most evil effect is that in denying the natural and rightful needs of the body it ultimately leads not only to the symbolic death of the lover—a common enough Petrarchan claim—but beyond this it causes the gradual extinction of the world and simultaneously of the lady herself by a death of his love and of his power to express that love.

> Therefore I'll give no more; But I'll undoe
> The world by dying; because love dies too.
> Then all your beauties will bee no more worth
> Then gold in Mines, where none doth draw it forth;
> And all your graces no more use shall have
>   Then a Sun dyall in a grave.
>   Thou Love taughtst mee, by making mee
> Love her, who doth neglect both mee and thee,
> To 'invent, and practise this one way, to 'annihilate
>   all three.

The poem extends the conventional motif in a novel and dramatic way, revealed by a comparison with Petrarch's poems on the same subject.

Sonnets XXXVIII, XLVII, and CXXIV portray Petrarch as fearing death caused by unrequited love. In the first he expects death as a direct consequence of Laura's disdain, for she has refused to grant him the life-giving force conveyed through her eyes which she scornfully lowers or covers with her hand. In the second sonnet he pleads with Laura to help him ward off the certain arrival of death by granting him her look and salute. In CXXIV he vents his amorous despair and voices his desire for death's solace, since love eats away his heart, fortune abandons it comfortless, and wrath poisons his mind. Sonnet XCV shows Petrarch introspectively meditating on Laura's perversity in not requiting him, while in sonnet XXXVI he first contemplates suicide as terminal relief for his suffering, but then renounces the idea with the excuse that the afterlife may simply be an extension of the present.[4]

> ma perch'io temo che sarrebbe un varco
> di pianto in pianto, et d'una in altra guerra,
> di qua dal passo anchor che mi si serra
> mezzo rimango, lasso, et mezzo il varco.[5]

In each poem Petrarch is content with giving lip-service to Laura's tormenting neglect and his inevitable death. His misery persists and so does his love with no indication that he can or is willing to do anything to alleviate it.

Although Petrarch calls on death to take him, he never treats the poetic motif literally as Donne does. While Petrarch contemplates that Laura's mistreatment " cagion sarà che 'nanzi tempo i'moia " (XXXVIII), in " The Will " Donne realistically dramatizes the lover's death as having already occurred or as near occurring, transforming a static poetic motif into an evolving literal event, a metaphorical gesture into a biographical fact, and thus actualizing Petrarchan conceits. The speaker of " The Will " is different from Petrarch. Undoubtedly, his Petrarchan quality is visible in his compulsion to love despite the possibility of death, in his suffering from the lady's denial of life-giving powers, and in the projection of his disillusionment to the outside world; but Donne's lover is not content with poetic verbalization about his inevitable death. Instead, he employs his death as a weapon of revenge, for he conceives the tactic of the will with its strange bequests as a way of dramatizing the cause and effects of his demise. The will is an active attempt to right the wrongs and injustices which would permit the perversity of his unnatural amorous condition. Typically, the speaker's attitude toward the world reflects his own disillusionment with love. As an example of a discontent Petrarchan lover who suffers denial, rejection, and imminent death, he generalizes his distrust and cynicism. For him the outside world has meaning only in direct proportion to the joy and fulfillment he experiences in love. (When Donne's speaker is a mutual lover, the injustices of the macrocosm are insignificant, and the world is simply a means for perpetuating the lovers' fame.) [6] The striking quality about this poem—that which distinguishes it from Petrarch's passive laments on the same subject—is that the speaker takes a detail common to an event of death in the real world, i.e., the will, and uses it within the context of his mythical world of love both to come to terms with his figurative death and as a way of setting aright through his legacies the evil of a world and of a lady who have dictated that he should love with no hope of reciprocity. Donne's lover, unlike Petrarch, not only accuses the lady of virtual homicide, but he also extends the ramifications of her denial to her, and through emotional blackmail he threatens love, and the world with personal retribution.

The visual quality of Petrarch's basic conceits and images facilitated their transfer into dramatically pictorial contexts, as in Donne's " The Funerall," where he begins with a Petrarchan image, transposes it to a highly dramatic scene, complicates its meaning, and at the end ironically inverts the original image. In " The Funerall " the lover imagines that he is already dead for love, and although the poems is intended as a description of his burial ceremony, its implications apply beyond the mere Petrarchan gesture of dying. It becomes a psychological meditation on the lady's " subtile wreath of haire."—what it means to him, what effects it has on him, and what the lady intended by giving it to him. In doing so the speaker tells a condensed story of the past, present, and future of his love, which we discover in stanza three was the cause of his death initially, while reversing the lady's salubrious effects conventionally affirmed in Petrarchan poetry. The overturning of this claim occurs gradually but deliberately. The lover at first has an ingenious but unfortunately inaccurate idea about the relic, asserting that, like his spinal cord which holds his body together in life, the lady's hair, as a symbol of his immortal soul, will preserve his body from dissolution after death. The life-giving powers of the Petrarchan lady alluded to so often in the *Canzoniere* are here attributed to a condition subsequent to death. But the speaker has fallen victim to deluding male self-projection. The opening lines of stanza one, especially the phrase " nor question much," suggest that the speaker is certain what the lock of hair means, but as the poem proceeds he begins to " question much " and to become less sure of his initial position. Toward the end of the second stanza he suddenly sees that his subjective interpretation of the relic's meaning may be at odds with what the lady really intended, and the speaker wonders...,

> Except she meant that I
> By this should know my pain,
> As prisoners then are manacled, when they'are condemned to die.

The relic turns from a symbol of the living, fertile quality of love and of the woman who gives it to a pernicious emblem of amorous imprisonment and then death, and thus, Donne ironically inverts the conventional Petrarchan notion of the lady's vitalizing abilities. Donne's speaker comes to see his lady as a member of the " dangerous sex," and the wreath assumes the same ambivalence for him as Pandora's box or Eve's apple did in past ages.

By creatively adapting stock love motifs, Donne presents in " The Funerall " a commentary on the emasculating nature of Petrarchan love. It is exposed as a denial of freedom by maintaining the lover in a perpetual state of unfulfilled desire. The lover's revised awareness of the hair's ambiguous meaning testifies to the deadening effects of this kind of love. He realizes that the wreath is intended to assure that the lover's condition after death will be as distressing as it was while he was alive— an adaptation of an idea Petrarch often acknowledges as in sonnet XXXVI—but Donne goes beyond the convention by making the lady directly responsible. The poem's dramatic effect derives not only from the vivid composition of place with which it opens—an imagined funeral scene with the lover laid out in his casket with a wreath of hair crowning his arm—but also from the pervading contrast between a love which gives life, as in " The Sunne Rising," and " The Good-morrow," and one which yields castrating death. This theme is further heightened by the darkening effect gradually intensified as the speaker's awareness grows. The poem's gloomy landscape is conveyed by the absence of words suggesting light, by the feeling of despair, and by the innocuous but sure movement from the open casket above the earth at the beginning to the closed casket below the earth at the end.

In the last stanza the speaker concludes that whatever its meaning or intention, it is best to bury the hair with him, since " it might breed/ idolatrie,/ If into others hands these Reliques came." His imagining of the physical death resulting from the lady's rejection is supplemented by his imagining of the revenge he will take on her because of her refusal to consummate the love, a further extension of Petrarchan conventions. But the revenge is ironic because first, it is questionable whether the act of burying a lock of hair is truly an effective revenge or a mere gesture, and second, the imagined revenge with its irreverent, not quite insulting tone, is intended as a veiled threat to the lady to convince her to submit. Thus, the lover still has hope. Finally, although the lover in truth has not died yet, he *sees* himself as dead, and thus we have the irony of a dead man fulfilling in his fictional revenge the " bravery " of sexual consummation denied him in life.

Expressed differently one could say that the poem traces the movement away from the effeminate " humility," obedience and submission of idealistic courtly adoration characteristic of Petrarchan love to the aggressive maleness (or " bravery ") of Ovidian love, a movement projected by the speaker's gradual awareness of the relic's ambivalent sexual implications. At first the relic is a " mystery " representing the ennobling quality of idealized love, for it miraculously preserves his body from disintegration; it represents the eternity of his love, for of all the parts of the body the hair is most resistent to dissolution; it represents life and continued virility in the face of death. But it also comes to symbolize his enslavement to the enigmatic yet powerfully attractive pleasure he knows the woman can give him; it personifies the satisfaction she has perversely denied him; and it is a reminder of his inescapable attachment to the claims of sexual desire. The bawdy implications are conveyed through the ambiguous overtones of such words as " arme," " haire," " sinewie thread," " bury," " wreath," and even

" outward Soule." The speaker cleverly conceals the sexual
connotations by his use of religious imagery in the first and
third stanzas, but the implications of his language emerge with
his use of quasi-anatomical imagery throughout, and then most
forcefully with the poem's last line in which the lover becomes
a partner to the homicidal activity he condemned in the lady,
" since you would save none of mee, I bury some of you." Sex
thus becomes a game of power, ascendancy, and domination
ultimately leading to conflict and death.

      " The Funerall " is a more hostile rendering of some of
the same motifs found in Donne's " The Relique," and the two
poems provide an interesting contrast for the treatment of the
Petrarchan death theme. In " The Relique " the speaker is
concerned with preserving love forever despite the death of the
body, while in " The Funerall " the speaker employs the
" dissolution " motif as an excuse for venting his anger at the
lady who is responsible for his sexual and physical death. The
speaker of " The Relique " looks forward to the survival and
discovery of the bracelet of hair in an age of misdevotion which
would worship these mutual lovers as saints. The bracelet is
not only a symbol of their eternal love and companionship, but
it also serves as a link between them and future generations. It
assures the lovers continuity despite their personal obliteration
by death. He is able to transcend the fact of death and anticipate
the fame assured by the future lovers who will imitate them.
The poem conveys a sense of the oneness of the lover and the
lady projected through the speaker's use of " wee " and " us,"
shifting only to the third person in the last line in order to
compliment her by way of the listener.[3] But the speaker of
" The Funerall " wants to bury the wreath of hair so that it
will not " breed idolatrie." Wishing to protect other lovers
from falling into the same trap as he, he hopes that future generations will not discover the relic. Captive of his physical desire,
he finds fame a poor compensation for death by deprivation.
The sense of oneness which begins the poem gives way to a
distinct separateness as he speaks in terms of " shee " and
" her " and then finally he uses the second person to voice his
proposed revenge. While the speaker of " The Relique " thinks

of survival and recovery, the lover in " The Funerall " sees only final death and absolute burial. In the one poem the lover transcends and conquers the immediacy of death and the claims of mortal life though his belief in fame; in the other the lover remains an unidentified, unreconciled, and unemulated victim of love's dying through female's castration.

In a more jocular tone " The Dampe " deals with the same theme as " The Funerall "—the lover's death resulting from the lady's perverse denial—but the tactic the speaker uses to resolve the problem is different. He asserts that the lady's rejection has effected an unnatural switching of their masculine and feminine roles, for she has become the conquering hero and the lover a begging slave. The poem focuses on the tension between how conventional, Petrarchan attitudes demand that the lover behave and what this lover's more masculine instincts are. It begins as Donne's other poems on this theme, dramatically with the speaker imagining himself dead at the lady's hands. The doctors, unsure of the cause of death, perform an autopsy and discover the lady's picture on his heart. The speaker anticipates that she will try to protect herself against such a discovery by working a similar death on them using " a sodaine dampe of love / ... and so preferre / Your murder, to the name of Massacre." The hyperbolic images point to the lady's multiplied killing power, but with subtle sexual overtones, and also to her selfishness and cruelty. In extending the lady's evil influence from the individual lovers to others, the speaker has both inverted and extended the Petrarchan idea of the lady's life-giving powers and ennobling effect.

In the second stanza the speaker deviates considerably from the conventional idea of the Petrarchan lady as powerful but essentially passive. Donne's lady in this poem is a brave, victorious knight, or better yet an Amazon, an image which better conveys the perversity of her actions, who travels the earth triumphing over men. In applying to her the exaggerated terminology of heroic feats—he combines battle allusions with those of destruction and death—the speaker actualizes what he believes to be her deviation from natural femininity. He advises her that before she kills others she should " First kill the'enormous Gyant, your *Disdaine,* / And let th'enchantress *Honor,* next be slaine." He compares her heroic acts to those of the barbarian Goths and Vandals who " Deface Records, and Histories " of their destructive " arts and triumphs." In this stanza Donne parodies Petrarch's technique of presenting a larger-than-life idealistic view of the lady, by offering instead an aggrandized image of the lady as a quasi-superhuman conqueror indiscriminately vanquishing her male opponents.

In the third stanza the lover regains his composure, asserting that he too could " muster up " his Giants and Witches against her feminist behavior. Ironically, the forces he would use to counteract the lady are those of idealized love —*Constancy* and *Secretness*—but he rejects them as a debasemènt of his manhood. He says that she would be more successful in " killing " him if she would use her " passive valor " rather than active heroics; that is, if she would be more like the original Petrarchan lady with one important exception, of course, she should submit

> doe you but try
> Your passive valor, and you shall finde than,
> Naked you'have odds enough of any man.

As a lesson on how best to " kill " the man, the last lines reject feminist activism while affirming woman's power over man through the clever manipulation of sex rather than open warfare between the sexes, since a man does not mind dying at a woman's hands if he can " die / As a meere man." [4] The speaker tries to convince his lady by arguing that she would have more power over him if she would requite his love, enslaving him to the source of his fulfillment. Of course, there has been a gradual redefinition of the words " death " and " kill " throughout the poem. Instead of merely lamenting his imminent death by denial at the lady's hands, Donne's speaker inverts the Petrarchan conceit by arguing that her seduction will in fact cause his death, and that is what she wanted in the first place.

The Petrarchan theme of death is one of Donne's favorites.[5] His treatment reveals the creative absorption and transformation of Petrarchanism, its themes and mode, for his own poetic purposes. The unique quality about Donne's approach to this theme is found in his use of ironic reversal whereby he explores and re-evaluates the nature and effects of Petrarchan love. His intention is to comment incisively on the aspect of Petrarchan love under scrutiny in a particular poem by the use of extension, exaggeration, and reversal of stock materials.

IX. DONNE'S PLACE
IN THE PETRARCHAN TRADITION:
A RETROSPECTIVE COMMENTARY

The most commonplace claim of Donne's critics—commonplace at least until the last fifteen or twenty years—has been that Donne was anti-Petrarchan and unconventional.[1] Praz, Guss, Andreasen, Stein[2] and a few others have attempted to modify this claim, each in a distinctive way. Duncan in *The Revival of Metaphysical Poetry* (New York, 1959) has carefully mapped out the road which has led to this point in Donne criticism. Donne fascinated early critics, such as Grosart and Gosse, most significantly as a man rather than as a poet. His early biographies reveal him as a mysterious, uniquely individual rebel and innovator whose poetry reflected his originality and devotion to a psychologically realistic portrayal of the world around him. Interpretations of Donne's personality were erroneously used as source material for analysis of his poetry. As an innovator and iconoclast, Donne was said to have purged post-Renaissance literature of stifling convention. Conceptions of Donne's originality based on psychological analysis significantly overlooked the fact that much of Donne's seeming uniqueness derived from the literary traditions—most specifically Petrarchanism—he was praised for repudiating.

Criticism based on personality was not the only problem. Eliot[3] and other poet-critics, in transferring their ideas on the creative act to critical interpretations of Donne, spoke of Donne's intellectualized emotion, of his ability to view an experience both emotionally and intellectually, of the dynamic relationship between thought and feeling in his poetry. Intent on making Donne a twentieth century man, they ignored the fact that his poetry offered a full expression of the tensions and complexities of that age to whose conventions he had certain access. Yet, despite the shortcomings of Eliot's criticism, much in his work has been the starting point for later scholars.

While others searched for points of difference to characterize the uniqueness of the metaphysicals from the poets of other ages, Eliot was one of the first to note their relationship to the Renaissance dramatists and the Italian poets of the *dolce stil nuovo*.

Subsequent concern about Donne's dramatic quality and use of literary analogues merely emphasized the inadequacies of early biographical criticism. Donne interpreters began to be interested in the poetic components of his work, in the poem's rhetorical situation, in the relationship of his poems to those of the same type in English and other languages, and in the significance of the critical theories and philosophical concepts of his age. Biographical criticism was especially helpless before the variety, and often contradictory, nature of Donne's treatment of love. More satisfactory answers regarding the contrarity of Donne's ideas were derived by analysis of his wit, rhetoric, and speaking voice.[4] Knowledge of the world picture and of the aesthetic theory prevalent in the Renaissance weighed heavily against conceptions of Donne as a unique poet. Donne was found to share a common ground with earlier Renaissance poets especially in his use of imagery and logic. If there was a difference it seemed to be in the fact that Elizabethan wit traced it origins back to Petrarch and the dolce stil nuovo while metaphysical wit turned on the discovery of ingenious analogies in nature and the universe.[5]

Donne's art reveals an orthodox exercise of the common 16th and 17th century practices of seeking knowledge of self and of the world by persistent witty reference to an objective and familiar known. Although Donne seems to have followed the practice of " correspondence " or universal analogy, the Petrarchan view of poetic inspiration which claimed that art was motivated by a love directed toward personal beauty was, nevertheless, an important factor in his love poetry. This is evident when Donne's poetic approach and amorous theory are compared to the gravely universalized and objective approach advocated by Giordano Bruno, who attempted to substitute erotic love with " heroic love " directed toward the universe. A cursory glance at the opening pages of Bruno's " Argomento del Nolano sopra Gli Eroici Furori " reveals both the substance and tone of Bruno's attack against Petrarchism, neither of which Donne ever approximates in his mature love poetry:

> E cosa veramente, o generosissimo Cavalliero,
> da basso, bruto et sporco ingegno, d'essersi
> fatto constantemente studioso, et aver affisso
> un curioso pensiero circa o sopra la bellezza
> d'un corpo femenile. Che spettacolo, o Dio
> buono!, più vile et ignobile può presentarsi
> ad un occhio di terso sentimento, che un uomo
> cogitabundo, afflitto, tormentato, triste,
> malinconioso; per dovenir or freddo, or caldo,
> or fervente, or tremante, or pallido, or rosso,
> or in mina di perplesso, or in atto di risoluto:
> un che spende il meglior intervallo di tempo et
> gli piú scelti frutti di sua vita corrente,
> destillando l'ELIXIR del cervello, con mettere
> in concetto, scritto, et sigillar in publichi
> monumenti, quelle continue torture, que' gravi
> tormenti, que' razionali discorsi, que' faticosi
> pensieri et quelli amarissimi studi destinati
> sotto la tirannide d'un indegna, imbecille,
> stolta et sozza sporcaria? [6]

The claim that Donne rejected the Petrarchan theory of poetic inspiration is qualified by a knowledge of how Donne adapted Petrarch's view of personal beauty and poetic inspiration by juxtaposing it against the correspondences perceived in the universe. Petrarch remains for the most part in a mythic poetic microcosm obsessed by his love for Laura's beauty, while Donne oscillates between the self-contained world of love and the time-ridden world of men.

This study has tried to show that although Donne could express himself within the limits of the Petrarchan vision, these limits did not detract from his originality nor did they prevent the inclusion of his own unique rearrangement of traditional themes. Donne's treatment of Petrarchan themes reveals his assimilation of poetic ideas and techniques and their creative re-use for new purposes. The relationship between his *Songs and Sonnets* and Petrarch is, therefore, not one of rejection but of absorption and reapplication. He shows an awareness that literary descriptions of amorous codes of behavior are not always consistent with the facts of reality or with human nature, but this does not necessarily mean for him that the ideal has no place in human experience. The dramatic use of speakers contributes to the projection of this awareness. Often the originality of his verse is accounted for by the tension he creates between the ideal and the real, between stereotyped attitudes, conceits, or situations and the lover's response to his individual predicament, between what he would like love to be and what it has in fact been. Sometimes Donne's vision includes the ideal with little actual modification either as an implied standard of comparison or as an accomplished reality, while at other times the code of Petrarchan love and behavior is extended beyond the original premises to its logical and often not so pleasant conclusions. Donne did not, as the pure imitators, did, stop with the superficialities of the Petrarchist tradition, nor did he repudiate Petrarch. He built on Petrarch, making his vision more relevant to practical experience. He used him as a catalyst to stimulate his own intellectual and poetic reaction to a conventional view of love, but the catalyst itself undergoes a change and is assimilated as an organic part of his work as Donne explores and extends its latent, unscrutinized possibilities. His cynicism and realism are inadequate explanations for his originality, just as they are inaccurate indices of his revolt, for his poetry is pervaded not so much by a feeling of repudiation as it is by a sense of curiosity, inclusion, balance, and adaptation.

" A Valediction: of my name in the Window " offers a summary example of how Donne assimilated the major themes and devices treated in this study.

> My name engrav'd herein,
> Doth contribute my firmnesse to this glasse,
> Which, ever since that charme, hath beene
> As hard, as that which grav'd it, was;
> Thine eyes will give it price enough, to mock
> The diamonds of either rock.

'Tis much that Glasse should bee
As all confessing, and through-shine as I,
    'Tis more, that it shewes thee to thee,
    And cleare reflects thee to thine eye.
But all such rules, loves magique can undoe,
    Here you see mee, and I am you.

        As no one point, nor dash,
Which are but accessarie to this name,
    The showers and tempests can outwash,
    So shall all times finde mee the same;
You this intirenesse better may fulfill,
    Who have the patterne with you still.

        Or if too hard and deepe
This learning be, for a scratch'd name to teach,
    It, as a given deaths head keepe,
    Lovers mortalitie to preach,
Or thinke this ragged bony name to bee
    My ruinous Anatomie.

        Then, as all my soules bee,
Emparadis'd in you, (in whom alone
    I understand, and grow and see,)
    The rafters of my body, bone
Being still with you, the Muscle, Sinew, 'and Veine,
    Which tile this house, will come againe.

        Till my returne repaire
And recompact my scatter'd body so,
    As all the vertuous powers which are
    Fix'd in the starres, are said to flow
Into such characters, as graved bee
    When those starres have supremacie,

        So since this name was cut
When love and griefe their exaltation had,
    No doore 'gainst this names influence shut;
    As much more loving, as more sad,
'Twill make thee; and thou shouldst, till I returne,
    Since I die daily, daily mourne.

        When thy'inconsiderate hand
Flings out this casement, with my trembling name,
    To looke on one, whose wit or land,
    New battry to thy heart may frame,
Then thinke this name alive, and that thou thus
    In it offendst my Genius.

> And when thy melted maid,
> Corrupted by thy Lover's gold, and page,
> His letter at thy pillow'hath laid,
> Disputed it, and tam'd thy rage,
> And thou begin'st to thaw towards him, for this,
> May my name step in, and hide his.

> And if this treason goe
> To'an overt act, and that thou write againe;
> In superscribing, this name flow
> Into thy fancy, from the pane.
> So, in forgetting thou remembrest right,
> And unaware to mee shalt write.

> But glasse, and lines must bee,
> No meanes our firme substantiall love to keepe;
> Neere death inflicts this lethargie,
> And this I murmure in my sleepe;
> Impute this idle talke, to that I goe,
> For dying men talke often so.

The parting situation dramatizes both the lover's conscious fear of the effect of separation on the lady and his hope that the written word can perpetuate and eternalize love. As a Petrarchan lover he recognizes the instability and inconstancy of human things, but, nevertheless, he seeks immortality and even fame for his love. He attempts to " anger Destiny " and assure the permanence of his love by means of a concrete relic. He engraves his name on her window, confident that the showers and tempests of life will never obliterate the living symbol of his love. The speaker's imaginings about the effect his engraved name will have on her while he is gone are motivated by his fundamental fear of her inconstancy. His evaluation of her ability to remain faithful and his imagining of fictional situations in stanzas eight, nine, and ten in which he foresees her infidelity are reminiscent of " Womans Constancy." But here the tone is more polite and restrained, less sarcastic and bitter, perhaps even a bit resigned. The lady needs some visible and inescapable reminder of the speaker's role in her life to secure her loyalty. His attitude toward her is ambivalent, for in one breath he exposes his Petrarchanism by implying that she is a goddess who fulfills his identity and assures him a meaningful life—an extension of Petrarch's idea that the lady holds the power to preserve or destroy the lover's world and that her eyes are the life-giving agents—while in another he fears that without the strength of his presence she may succumb to temptation. She is regarded simultaneously as a goddess on a pedestal, as an equal partner in the love relationship, and as the weaker sex needing masculine guidance. He does not doubt that she loves him now, but his fears for the future motivate his attempt to preserve the integrity of the love. The lovers have exchanged hearts, but the speaker's anxiety suggests that the lady has accepted his heart only temporarily. He is a cautious idealist clinging to a romantic view of love but well aware of the more realistic alternatives. He knows that parting could result in physical death by some accident during the journey, or worse, in a figurative death of love.

In the event of either possibility the name is to exert a magical influence, not unlike that of the " Booke " in " Valediction: of the Booke," for as she gazes on the glass " loves magique " will make her see his image rather than her own. The image of the mirroring glass is a transmogrification of the Petrarchan image of the eyes reflecting the beloved. At the same time the lover hopes that the name will incite her to mourn daily, a curious wish since in other valediction poems, where the love is " substantiall," the lover forbids mourning, or consoles the lady's mourning, as in " Sweetest love," or fears her mourning as a cause of his death, as in " Valediction: of Weeping." Yet the speaker's ambiguous use of the language and imagery of death in stanzas four through seven coupled with the vividness of his fantasizing about her possible betrayal undercut the name's positive effect. The final repudiation of the name in the last stanza as the " idle talke " of a dying man is one example of the frequent shifts in tone occurring at crucial points in the poem (stanzas one through three express one tone, four through seven another, eight through ten another, and eleven another), and contributes to the effect of uncertainty and insecurity. The name is at once a symbol of the lover's fidelity, an objectification of his mortal remains, and a reminder of love's most evil effects, grief and death. But in the end he realizes his own self-deception, for symbols are only symbols; they cannot in fact resurrect a dead man, and their true value resides in the humans who do or do not observe their meanings. In exploring the Petrarchan solution to the question of love's permanence, the speaker concludes that however admirable they are, poetry and fame can neither assure the eternity of love nor compensate for a joyless and unfulfilling love: " glasse, and lines must bee, / No meanes our firme substantiall love to keepe."

Moreover, the poem presents an evaluation of the effectiveness of the Petrarchan idea of the imagination. The speaker fears that the lady will be unable to survive separation assisted only by the evoking powers of the mind. Recollection and thought of the beloved may temporarily soothe the grief of separation or of actual death, but humans cannot live forever on memory and contemplation, and soon both are replaced by the impelling activities and temptations of daily existence. The imaginative act of remembering cannot substitute for the lover's actual presence. Thus, the speaker's claim in the last stanza that he is physically dying is a figurative gesture, for the kind of death he has really been talking about in the poem is the death of love, for which fame is certainly no remedy.

" A Valediction: of my name in the Window " demonstrates how Donne can be " Petrarchan," without being " Petrarchist." [7] He was neither a pure imitator of Petrarch nor a pure reactionary against him.[8] His poems do not conform to the superficial literary manner of either extreme school, but they are an attempt to renovate exhausted but valuable Petrarchan modes. His treatment of the Petrarchan vision of love is complex because he combines the apotheosis of woman and constancy of the Petrarchan mode with the flesh and blood experiences of the aggressive lover. He redefines the Neoplatonic worship of woman as an incarnation of beauty in terms of how man can tangibly enjoy and possess this beauty. In short, Donne's variation of Petrarchan themes is unique because it exemplifies so well the Elizabethan age's " curious conception of love as at once a high social convention and a vivid personal experience." [9]

NOTES

Chapter I, The Unwanted Heart

¹ See C. S. Lewis, " Donne and Love Poetry in the Seventeenth Century," *John Donne: A Collection of Critical Essays*, ed. Helen Gardner (Englewood Cliffs, 1965), pp. 90-99; Patricia Garland Pinka, " The Voices in John Donne's *Songs and Sonets*," unpublished dissertation, University of Pittsburgh (June, 1969); Lowry Nelson, Jr., *Baroque Lyric Poetry* (New Haven, 1961); N. J. D. Andreasen, *John Donne: Conservative Revolutionary* (Princeton, 1967); Donald Guss, *John Donne, Petrarchist* (Detroit, 1966); H. M. Richmond, " Ronsard and the English Renaissance," *Comparative Literature Studies*, VII (June 1970), 141-159.

² All citations of Petrarch's *Canzoniere* refer to Francesco Petrarca, *Canzoniere*, ed. Gianfranco Contini and Daniele Ponchiroli (Torino, 1968).

³ " Castelvetro says that it is commonly (though wrongly) believed that Petrarch's ' Mira quel colle ' is a dialogue between Petrarch, who wants to go, and his heart, who wants to stay. Such a belief would emphasize the parallels between Petrarch's sonnet and ' The Blossom '." Guss, *Petrarchist*, p. 205.

⁴ All citations of Donne's *Songs and Sonets* refer to *The Elegies and The Songs and Sonnets*, ed. Helen Gardner (London, 1965).

⁵ *Ibid.*, p. 219.

⁶ There is also the suggestion of the contrast between " ideal " and " real " in these two words.

⁷ Pinka says that the topical metaphors which the speaker uses for analogy—death by plague and burning flash of powder—are transmogrifications of the Petrarchan conceits of burning and freezing for love. " The Voices in John Donne's *Songs and Sonets*," p. 87.

⁸ One recalls Petrarch's line in sonnet CCXXI, " et son già ardendo nel vigesimo anno."

Chapter II, Donne's ' Parody ' of the Petrarchan Lady

¹ See sonnets CLX and CLXV for examples. With a few exceptions, Donne's women are of the " indoor " type.

² For additional information on the relationship of Petrarch to the Provençal, Sicilian, and Tuscan love schools, see Mariateresa Cattaneo, *Francesco Petrarca e la lirica d'arte del '200* (Torino, 1964), pp. v-xvi; Baldo Curato, *Introduzione a Petrarca* (Cremona, 1963), pp. 174-241; Gianfranco Contini, " Preliminari sulla lingua del Petrarca," *Francesco Petrarca, Canzoniere* (Torino, 1968), pp. vii-xxxviii; Carlo Calcaterra, " Il Petrarca e il petrarchismo," *Questioni e correnti di storia letteraria* (Milano, 1968), p. 172.

[3] Frederick Goldin, *The Mirror of Narcissus* (Ithaca, 1967), p. 14.

[4] Calcaterra points out that the characteristic quality of Petrarch's contribution to literary history, a quality his successors would attempt to imitate, is his dramatization of love as a conflict between reality and ideal. " Il Petrarca e il petrarchismo," p. 200. It is in the extension and development of this essentially Petrarchan quality that Donne makes a significant contribution to the Petrarchist tradition.

[5] Goldin, *The Mirror of Narcissus*, p. 82.

[6] See *The Poems of John Donne*, ed. H. J. C. Grierson, II (Oxford, 1912), xi-xii, as one example.

[7] See Patricia Pinka, " The Voices in John Donne's *Song and Sonets*," pp. 155-157 for a discussion of Donne's " Dreaming Cynics."

[8] Douglas L. Peterson, *The English Lyric From Wyatt to Donne* (Princeton, 1967), p. 297.

[9] Goldin, *The Mirror of Narcissus*, p. 87.

[10] Alvin Kernan, *The Cankered Muse: Satire of the English Renaissance* (New Haven, 1959), p. 250).

[11] Gilbert Highet, *The Anatomy of Satire* (Princeton, 1962), p. 10.

[12] Clay Hunt, *Donne's Poetry* (New Haven, 1962), pp. 2-3 and p. 6.

[13] Highet, *The Anatomy of Satire*, p. 105.

Chapter III, Amorous Abberrations

[1] See canzone LXXI, LXXII, and sonnets CXL and CLXIII for other examples of love's virtuous effects.

[2] Lu Emily Pearson, *Elizabethan Love Conventions* (New York, 1966 rep.), pp. 224-228.

[3] In sonnet XVII Petrarch laments his separation from Laura's eyes which direct his life, as the stars influence the planets.

[4] The word " falls " in line eight has a negative connotation in reference to the lady, perhaps suggesting, as Empson says, the lady's " falling " into infidelity. " A Valediction: Of Weeping," *John Donne: A Collection of Critical Essays*, ed. Helen Gardner, pp. 53-54.

[5] This is unlike the claim in " Valediction: forbidding mourning " where the lovers experience " an expansion " in separation, and are kept together " as stiffe twin compasses " are kept together.

[6] Petrarch's sonnet XVII compares his sighs to a " tormenting wind."

[7] Donne repeats this idea in " Sweetest love: I doe not goe," in which the lover warns that the lady does the lover harm by sighing and weeping so much, and that her " divining heart," which imagines all kinds of tragedies occurring on his trip, may by its very imaginings contribute to his misfortune, if Destiny listen to her.

[8] Gardner, *The Elegies and the Songs and Sonnets*, p. 215. See Andreasen's comment on the religious derivation of this image. *Conservative Revolutionary* (Princeton, 1967), pp. 146-147.

[9] T. H. White, ed. *The Bestiary* (New York, 1960), p. 191.

[10] There is a difference between the speakers of " Communitie " and " Confined Love," whose fables are designed to be taken as sincere and serious assertions of their love philosophy, and the speaker of " Loves Diet," whose

fable does not have such an intention. This fact is substantiated by the speaker's deep resentment over the lady's infidelity, by the poem's implicit comparisons with the Petrarchan ideal, by his repeated use of " I " indicating personal involvement and commitment, and by the " diet " conceit itself which is a course of action used to remedy overindulgence.

[11] This folly is dramatically pointed to in sonnet CCLXVI, the last written in Laura's life:

> Poi quel dolce desio ch'Amor mi spira
> menami a morte, ch'i' non me n'aveggio;
>
> . . . .
>
> Carità di signore, amor di donna
> son le catene ove con molti affanni
> legato son, perch'io stesso mi strinsi.

[12] For a discussion of how the lover and alchemist are alike in their respective quests see Edgar H. Duncan, " Donne's Alchemical Figures," *Discussions of John Donne* (New York, 1962), p. 74.

[13] Edgar Duncan rightly points out that in other poems Donne often presents the positive sides of alchemy. For example, the theories surrounding gold are used positively in " Valediction: forbidding Mourning " and in *The Anniversaries*, where gold serves as an analogy for Elizabeth Drury. " Donne's Alchemical Figures," pp. 76-89.

[14] The language here recalls Dante's description of the carnal sinners in the fifth canto of the *Inferno*.

Chapter IV, Dreams, Memories, and Fantasies

[1] Frederick Goldin, *The Mirror of Narcissus in the Courtly Love Lyric*, pp. 83-85. Goldin implies that the imagination is a kind of mirror, " an instrument of illusions, barren of every attribute except its ability to reflect what is set before it in such a way that the image seems real . . . yet it gives to the soul its first captivating glimpse of the ideal." (p. 14). Cattaneo attributes the mythical quality of Laura's portrayal to Petrarch's use of memory, dream, and imagination. *Francesco Petrarca e la lirica d'arte del '200* (Torino, 1964), p. xii. For additional information about the function of imagination in creating the so-called " mito fantastico dell'amore per Laura," see Natalino Sapegno, *Dalle rime e dai Trionfi e dalle opere minori latine di Francesco Petrarca* (Florence, 1962), pp. 909-911, and Fausto Montanari, *Studi sul Canzoniere del Petrarca* (Roma, 1958), pp. 134-135.

[2] The function of the imagination in changing or affecting the world of love can be compared to the Renaissance view, as expressed for example, by Sidney in his *Apology for Poetry*, of how art (the golden world) can influence the world of reality (the brazen world). The imagination as an instrument of art was considered as a preeminent and necessary faculty for the effective poet in projecting his " feigned example."

Yet it was also thought that the imagination could distort and misconstrue information supplied by the senses, and as a consequence, by upsetting the balance of humors could cause great confusion in the body and mind. To the Renaissance moral philosopher the imagination was notoriously suspect for it could ". . . .make new configurations of its own that have no reference to

" It could produce, as in Donne's " The Apparition," dreams, visions,
demons, monstrous sights that could cause madness. " Although it was
ughest faculty of animals, in man it should be under the surveillance and
pline of the understanding, and be like a mirror to give a true reflection
externals." Herschel Baker, *The Image of Man* (New York, 1947), pp. 283-
5. A number of Renaissance treatises consider the nature and effects of the
nagination. Consult Bacon's *Advancement of Learning*, Book II; Greville's
A *Treatise of Humane Learning*, Burton's *Anatomy*, and La Primaudaye's *The
French Academie*.

   [3] Arnold Stein, *The Eloquence of Action* (Minneapolis, 1962), p. 190.
Also, see what Patricia Pinka says about this subject. " The Voices in John
Donne's *Songs and Sonets*," p. 88.

   [4] In Petrarch's poem it is the lady who haunts the lover—the reverse
of Donne's poem—a detail which stresses the lover's passivity. These Petrarchan
analogues suggest that Petrarch is driven to desire revenge by scornful treatment,
even though he may not perhaps express the delight of Donne's speaker at
the lady's anticipated torments.

   [5] Helen Gardner, *The Elegies and The Songs and Sonnets*, pp. xxi-xxii.

   [6] However, this realization appears side by side with a similar awareness
in Petrarch of love's evil effects. Once more this indicates Petrarch's vacillation
and contradiction, a confirmation of the judgment some critics have made that
" l'amore petrarchesco è sopra tutto in conflitto con se stesso." Carlo Calcaterra,
" Il Petrarca e il petrarchismo," *Questioni e correnti di storia letteraria*, pp.
174-175.

   [7] Grierson prefers " truth " to " true," ". . . she is ' truth ' as opposed
to dreams or phantasms or aught that partakes of unreality. She is essentially
truth as God is. . . ." *The Poems of John Donne*, II, p. 35.

Chapter V, Suns and Lovers

   [1] The sexual overtones in Petrarch's language have been substantially
ignored or rationalized in traditional criticism. See Umberto Bosco, *Francesco
Petrarca* (Bari, 1965), pp. 15-53; Ettore Bonora, " Francesco Petrarca," *I classici italiani nella storia della critica*, I, ed. Walter Binni (Florence, 1970), pp.
101-165; Baldo Curato, *Introduzione a Petrarca*, pp. 174-241. In his fine study
on European Petrarchism Leonard Forster says that the *alba* was " the
crowning triumph of a long siege to a lady's heart." *The Icy Fire* (Cambridge,
1969), p. 87. Forster points out that the *alba* form usually sang in elegiac tone
of a lover's secret and frustrated passion for a hard-hearted, withholding lady,
but that ultimately his desire is requited. This view is substantiated by Peter
Dronke in *The Medieval Lyric* (New York, 1968), pp. 167-185, who comments
further that the *alba*, one of the kind of " songs that grew out of imagined
events," usually portrayed the lover as having already gained the woman's love.
Both these conventions suggest interesting possibilities when applied to
Petrarch. Forster states that the *alba* functioned as " a safety valve for repressed
sensual desire," requiring that love and its consummation remain secret and
sexual union in poetry be treated discretely. Forster, *The Icy Fire*, pp. 85-86.
In sonnet CCXIX Petrarch follows this practice by camouflaging his meaning
through the use of metaphors and classical mythology. Although Forster treats

the conventions of the *alba*, he does not deal to any great extent with the thematic elements common to the form—the lovers' relationship to time and the world—which I treat later in this essay. Dronke shows how these themes operate in the medieval *alba*.

[2] Robert Graves points out the negative associations of the Dawn-maiden's constant love affairs with young men, commenting further that her story is more of an allegory than a myth of how " dawn brings midnight lovers a renewal of erotic passion, and is the most usual time for men to be carried off by fever." *The Greek Myths*, I (Baltimore, 1961), p. 150. It well may be that Petrarch uses the story for the same allegorical purpose.

[3] " Tithonus has been taken by the allegorist to mean 'a grant of a stretching-out..., a reference to the stretching-out of his life, at Eos's plea; but it is likely, rather, to have been a masculine form of Eos's own name, Titone—from *tito*, ' day ' ... and *one*, ' queen '—to have meant ' partner of the Queen of Day '," *The Greek Myths*, p. 150. In paralleling his love situation to that in the myth, Petrarch sees himself, as Tithonus was, the partner of Laura, the Queen of Day.

[4] The mundane pedants, tardy school boys, etc. would equate with Petrarch's birds as dawn harbingers.

[5] Peter Dronke's *The Medieval Lyric*, p. 168 was most helpful in identifying this convention of the *alba*.

[6] The medieval *alba* often begins with an invocation to God. Dronke, *The Medieval Lyric*, p. 176. In Petrarch and Donne the sun is directly substituted for God.

Chapter VI, Petrarchan Imagery in " The Canonization "

[1] An obvious example would be Cleanth Brooks' analysis of the poem in chapter one of *The Well Wrought Urn* (New York, 1947).

[2] See Donald Guss, *John Donne, Petrarchist*, pp. 155-159. With a few scattered exceptions, it is Guss' general concern to relate Donne to the imitators of Petrarch rather than to Petrarch himself. Although Guss cites some of the Petrarchan analogues for the images in " The Canonization," he does not show how Petrarch's use differs from Donne's. He is concerned with proving how the poem is an example of Donne's Neoplatonic posture by referring mostly to Italian philosophical tracts on the subject: thus, he only briefly acknowledges some of the Petrarchan images in Donne without developing the cross-references.

[3] In her commentary on the poem, Helen Gardner says, " The comparison of lovers to a butterfly attracted to its death by the flame of a candle derives ultimately from Petrarch." *The Elegies and The Songs and Sonnets*, p. 203.

[4] Petrarch may be alluding here to the myth of the eagle, who when he grows old and " his wings become heavy and his eyes become darkened with a mist, then he goes in search of a fountain, and over against it, he flies up to the height of heaven, even unto the circle of the sun; and there he singes his wings and at the same time evaporates the fog of his eyes, in a ray of the sun. Then at length, taking a header down into the fountain, he dips himself three times in it, and instantly he is renewed with a great vigour of plumage and

splendor of vision." In the mythic stories told about the eagle it is claimed that he possessed a fearless and acute eyesight along with the uninjured power of staring directly into the sun's rays. T. H. White, ed., *The Bestiary*, pp. 105-107.

[5] Guss says that this sonnet informs Donne's use of the image of " the eagle who stares fixedly at the sun, and so represents the lover whose eyes are fixed on the lady." *John Donne, Petrarchist*, p. 199. An analysis of the sonnet reveals, however, that Petrarch does not associate himself with the eagle at all, but with the moth consumed by the fire of passion.

[6] It should be noted that in sonnets XXV and XXVI Petrarch, like Donne's speaker of " The Canonization," also defends the amorous life, especially praising a friend who after a long absence from his poetic art, returns to his singing of love's joys and sorrows. Donne's poem, specifically what is said in stanza four, indicates that it not only justifies the amorous life, but love poetry itself as in Petrarch.

[7] Guss has pointed out the Petrarchan analogue but not demonstrated how the function of the image differs in Donne. For a general survey of the phoenix image in Renaissance literature, see Marc-René Jung, *Etudes sur le poeme allegorique en France* (Berne, 1971), pp. 220-226, Jean Hubaux and Maxim Leroy, *Le mythe du phenix dans les litteratures grecque et latine* (Paris, 1939), and Marion Kaplan, *The Phoenix in Elizabethan Poetry*, unpublished dissertation, University of California, 1964.

[8] In sonnet CLXXXV Petrarch uses the phoenix analogy to describe Laura's beauty, while in sonnet CLXIX Petrarch refers to Laura as his " darling dove." This relates to Donne's use of the dove in " The Canonization " to represent the feminine principle.

[9] This is Donne's creative reshaping of Petrarch's ideas on fame, self-eternalization, artistic recognition and reward. We find Donne exploring these mostly in " The Triple Foole," " The Undertaking," " The Relique," among others. When Donne's speaker is a denied Petrarchan lover, then, like Petrarch, he sees poetry as a vent for amorous frustration, and fame becomes a substitute for the acceptance and fulfillment refused him by the lady.

[10] *Ugo Foscolo, Poesie e Prose Scelte*, ed. Gustavo Rodolfo Ceriello (Milano, 1947), p. 88.

Chapter VII, Fools, Heroes, and Saints: The Petrarchan Hope for Fame

[1] Benedetto Croce, *Poesia popolare e poesia d'arte* (Bari, reprinted 1967), p. 66.

[2] *The Anniversaries* offer additional material for a study of how Donne varied Petrarchan fame motifs. But Donne's treatment there should be viewed within the elegiac, rather than the amorous context only, and *The Anniversaries* should be considered in relation to Petrarch's sonnets written after Laura's death. Evidence of Donne's religious attitude toward fame appears in his other works, as for example, in the *Essays in Divinity*.

[3] For an extended study of Petrarch's sense of the " caducità della vita... di ogni cosa viva," and how it relates to his ideas of love and to his conception of Laura, see Umberto Bosco, *Francesco Petrarca* (Bari, 1965), pp. 54-67. Bosco

points out that although the themes of love and of the labile quality of earthly existence are closely allied, it would be erroneous to reduce one to the other. *Ibid.*, p. 83. Love, fame, and death are all closely related aspects of Petrarch's vision of life and love.

Chapter VIII, Ironic Reversal of Petrarchan Death Motifs

[1] I would agree with Professor Forster's statement: " ... the attacks (by the so-called anti-Petrarchists) never seriously called in doubt the validity of the convention or its usefulness as a means of poetic expression; they came from within the convention itself. ' Anti-petrarchism ' is thus only an aspect of petrarchism." Later Professor Forster says, " It is noticeable that some of the most outspoken anti-petrarchists are also among the successful petrarchists— du Bellay, and even Sidney and Shakespeare. Just as you cannot live for ever on strawberries and cream, so you cannot maintain the mood of true Petrarchan or Neoplatonic exaltation for very long (though Petrarch could, but then he was a very unusual person). You can, however, go on using the convention for your own purposes." *The Icy Fire*, p. 66. I would include Donne in the list of anti-petrarchists, successful as a petrarchist.

[2] See Forster's discussion of life-death themes and images in Petrarch and later writers. Forster, *The Icy Fire*, pp. 19-20.

[3] See chapter VII for a more extensive treatment of " The Relique."

[4] Donne's lines suggest the contradictory attitude found in Petrarch, that it is death to be separated from his lady, as in sonnet XVII, and it is death to be joined to the lady, as in sonnet XVIII. In " The Dampe " Donne's speaker prefers the latter.

[5] In addition to the poems discussed in this chapter, the theme is also explored uniquely in " The Feaver," " The Dissolution," and " The Nocturnall." We can safely say that Donne employs ironic reversal in them as well to re-evaluate Petrarchan claims.

Chapter IX, Donne's Place in Petrarchan Tradition: A Retrospective Commentary

[1] " Donne's treatment of love is entirely unconventional except when he chooses to dally half ironically with the convention of Petrarchan adoration." H. J. C. Grierson, " Metaphysical Poetry," *Metaphysical Lyrics and Poems of the Seventeenth Century* (Oxford, 1921), p. 7. While Grierson was asserting the unconventional quality of Donne's love treatment and his " new psychological curiosity " he was at the same time acknowledging the indebtedness of his metaphysical wit and imagery to the " concetti metafisici ed ideali " of the dolce stil nuovo school.

[2] Mario Praz, *The Flaming Heart* (Gloucester, 1966); Guss, *The Petrarchist*; Andreasen, *John Donne: Conservative Revolutionary*; Arnold Sein, *John Donne's Lyrics: The Eloquence of Action* (Minneapolis, 1962).

[3] T. S. Eliot, " The Metaphysical Poets," *Selected Essays, 1917-1932* (New York, 1921).

[4] Stein says that Donne's originality derives from his " invention "—his

personal rearrangement of aspects available to his predecessors—in his recognition and development of the latent possibilities of a subject while observing conventional rules. *The Eloquence of Action*, pp. 87-88.

[5] For views on wit consult Rosemond Tuve, *Elizabethan and Metaphysical Imagery* (Chicago, 1947); S. L. Bethell, " The Nature of Metaphysical Wit," *Discussions of John Donne* (Boston, 1962), pp. 136-149; and J. A. Mazzeo, " Metaphysical Poetry and the Poetic of Correspondences," *Journal of the History of Ideas*, XV, (1955), pp. 223-232.

[6] Giordano Bruno, *De Gl' Heroici Furori*, ed. Francesco Flora, (Torino, 1928), p. 3. " ... Giordano Bruno offre curioso ma non inesplicabile esempio di un violento antipetrarchismo programmatico e teorico, coesistente con l'assimilazione e l'adozione di caratteristici modi stilistici desunti dal Petrarca e dai petrarchisti... Incomprensione che ci riuscirà meno incomprensibile ove si pensi che l'odio bruniano per i ' regolisti di poesia,' per ' gli pedanti ' e per i ' grammatisti invecchiati nelle culine de fanciulli et notomie de frasi et de vocabuli, lo ha probabilmente portato a confondere in un'unica condanna gl'imitatori servili e l'incolpevole modello '." B. T. Sozzi, *Petrarca* (Palermo, 1963), p. 41.

[7] " *Petrarchismo* is the art of treating cleverly and wittily matters of the heart, of composing love-poems without the emotion in the soul, of feigning passion for an imaginary mistress, and of singing a fiction of amorous intrigue, whose phases and whose stages are fixed, and as it were, established by an immovable tradition. To succeed in this type our sixteenth-century poets needed only a little learning and imagination, a great deal of memory, and a certain ability in the art of composition." John M. Berdan, " A Definition of Petrarchismo," *PMLA*, XXIV (Dec. 1909), p. 704, as quoted from Marius Pieri, *Petrarque et Ronsard*.

[8] Mario Praz points out that Bembo's reaction against degenerated forms of Petrarchism took the form of a return to Petrarch, the poet, not to Petrarch, the occasional mannerist. *The Flaming Heart* (Gloucester, 1966), p. 270.

[9] Alden, " The Lyrical Conceit of the Elizabethans," *Studies in Philology*, XIV (1917), p. 152.

BIBLIOGRAPHY

Alden, Raymond MacDonald. " The Lyrical Conceit of the Elizabethans," *Studies in Philology*, XIV (1917), 129-152.

Andreasen, N. J. D. *John Donne: Conservative Revolutionary*. Princeton, 1967.

Baker, Herschel. *The Image of Man*. New York, 1947.

Baldacci, Luigi. *Il petrarchismo italiano nel Cinquecento*. Milano, 1957.

Berdan, John M. " A Definition of Petrarchismo," *PMLA*, XXIV (December 1909), 701-710.

Bergin, Thomas G. *Petrarch's Bucolicum Carmen*. New Haven, 1974.

Bonora, Ettore. " Francesco Petrarca," *I classici italiani nella storia della critica*, I, ed. Walter Binni. Firenze, 1970.

Bosco, Umberto. *Francesco Petrarca*. Bari, 1965.

Brooks, Cleanth. *The Well Wrought Urn*. New York, 1947.

Bruno, Giordano. *De Gl'Heroici Furori*, ed. Francesco Flora. Torino, 1928.

Calcaterra, Carlo. " Il Petrarca e il petrarchismo," *Questioni e correnti di storia letteraria*. Milano, 1968.

Cappuccio, Carmelo. *Poeti e prosatori italiani*. Milano, 1960.

Cattaneo, Mariateresa. *Francesco Petrarca e la lirica d'arte del '200*. Torino, 1964.

Croce, Benedetto. *Poesia popolare e poesia d'arte*. Bari, 1967 rep.

Curato, Baldo. *Introduzione a Petrarca*. Cremona, 1963.

De Sanctis, Francesco. " Il *Canzoniere*," *Storia della letteratura italiana*, ed. Benedetto Croce. Bari, 1954, pp. 262-273.

Donne, John. *The Poems of John Donne*, ed. H. J. C. Grierson. 2 vols. Oxford, 1912.

—. *The Elegies and The Songs and Sonnets*, ed. Helen Gardner. London, 1965.

Dronke, Peter. *The Medieval Lyric*. New York, 1968.

Duncan, Joseph E. *The Revival of Metaphysical Poetry*. New York, 1959.

Eliot, T. S. " The Metaphysical Poets," *Selected Essays*, 1917-1932. New York, 1921.

England, George Allan. " Feministic and Literary Influences of Petrarchanism," *Poet Lore*, XXVIII (1917), 187-216.

Forster, Leonard. *The Icy Fire*. Cambridge, 1969.

Foscolo, Ugo. *Poesie e Prose Scelte*, ed. Gustavo Rodolfo Cericello. Milano, 1947.

—. *Saggi sopra il Petrarca*, ed. G. Papini. Lanciano, Carabba, 1911.

Frye, Northrop. *Anatomy of Criticism.* Princeton, 1957.

Gardner, Helen, ed. *John Donne: A Collection of Critical Essay.* Englewood Cliffs, 1965.

Goldin, Frederick. *The Mirror of Narcissus.* Ithaca, 1967.

Graves, Robert. *The Greek Myths.* 2 vols. Baltimore, 1961.

Grierson, H. J. C. " Metaphysical Poetry," *Metaphysical Lyrics and Poems of the Seventeenth Century.* Oxford, 1921.

Guss, Donald. *John Donne, Petrarchist.* Detroit, 1966.

Highet, Gilbert. *The Anatomy of Satire.* Princeton, 1962.

Hollway-Calthrop, H. C. *Petrarch: His Life and Times.* New York, 1972 rep.

Hubaux, Jean and Leroy, Maxim. *Le mythe du phenix dans les litteratures grecque et latine.* Paris, 1939.

Hunt, Clay. *Donne's Poetry.* New Haven, 1962.

Jung, Marc-Renè. *Etudes sur le poeme allegorique en France.* Berne, 1971.

Kaplan, Marion. *The Phoenix in Elizabethan Poetry*, unpublished dissertation. University of California, 1964.

Kermode, Frank, ed. *Discussions of John Donne.* Boston, 1962.

Kernan, Alvin. *The Cankered Muse: Satire of the English Renaissance.* New Haven, 1959.

Lea, K. M. " Conceits," *Modern Language Review*, XX (October 1925), 389-406.

Leishman, J. B. *The Monarch of Wit.* New York, 1951.

Mazzeo, Joseph Anthony. " Metaphysical Poetry and the Poetic of Correspondences," *Journal of the History of Ideas*, XV (1955), 223-232.

Miner, Earl. *Seventeenth-Century Imagery.* Berkeley, 1971.

Montanari, Fausto. *Studi sul Canzoniere del Petrarca.* Roma, 1958.

Morley, Lord (Henry Parker). *Tryumphes of Fraunces Petrarke*, ed. D. D. Carnicelli. Cambridge, 1971.

Nelson, Lowry, Jr. *Baroque Lyric Poetry.* New Haven, 1961.

Noferi, Adelia. *L'esperienza poetica del Petrarca.* Firenze, 1962.

Pearson, Lu Emily. *Elizabethan Love Conventions.* New York, 1966 rep.

Peterson, Douglas L. *The English Lyric From Wyatt to Donne.* Princeton, 1967.

Petrarca, Francesco. *Canzoniere*, ed. Gianfranco Contini and Daniele Ponchiroli. Torino, 1968.

—. *Le Rime*, ed. Giosuè Carducci and Severino Ferrari. Firenze, 1899.

—. *Letters From Petrarch*, ed. Morris Bishop. Bloomington, 1966.

Pinka, Patricia Garland. " The Voices in John Donne's *Songs and Sonets*," unpublished dissertation, University of Pittsburgh (June, 1969).

Richmond, H. M. " The Intangible Mistress," *Modern Philology*, LVI (May 1959), 217-223.

—. " Ronsard and the English Renaissance," *Comparative Literature Studies*, VII (June 1970), 141-159.

Russo, Luigi. " Il Petrarca e il Petrarchismo," *Belfagor*, IX (1954).

—. *Ritratti e disegni storici.* Firenze, 1960.

Sanders, Wilbur. *John Donne's Poetry.* Cambridge, 1971.

Sapegno, Natalino. *Dalle rime e dai Trionfi e dalle opere minori latine di Francesco Petrarca.* Firenze, 1962.

—. *Il Trecento.* Milano, 1953.

Sharp, Robert Lothrop. *From Donne to Dryden.* Hamden, Conn., 1940.

Smith, A. J. " Donald Guss's *John Donne, Petrarchist,*" *Renaissance Quarterly* (Summer 1968), 231-233.

Sozzi, B. T. *Petrarca.* Palermo, 1963.

Spagnoletti, Giacinto. *Il petrarchismo.* Milano, 1959.

Stein, Arnold. *The Eloquence of Action.* Minneapolis, 1962.

Tuve, Rosemond. *Elizabethan and Metaphysical Imagery.* Chicago, 1947.

—. " 'Sacred Parody' of Love Poetry, and Herbert," *Studies in the Renaissance*, VIII (1961), 249-286.

Valency, Maurice. *In Praise of Love.* New York, 1958.

White, T. H. ed. *The Bestiary.* New York, 1960.

Whitefield, J. H. *Petrarca e il Rinascimento.* Bari, 1949.

Wilkens, Ernest Hatch. *Life of Petrarch.* Chicago, 1961.

—. *The Making of the Canzoniere.* Roma, 1951.

INDEX

References to Donne, Petrarch and Laura have not been indexed because of their numerous frequency.